Praise

Insatiable

An extraordinary exploration into the relentless pursuit of excellence. With profound insight, Martínez Denia illuminates the path from self-sabotage to self-mastery, offering leaders a transformative journey toward achieving unparalleled performance and unlocking their freedom to become their own greatest ally. A must-read for any leader striving to transcend their limitations and harness their full potential – for the good of the organizations and people depending on them as well as their own.

Dr. Thorsten Reiter, author of *Killing Innovation*

This powerful book for leaders presents timely and actionable perspectives that directly address the current complex times we are all facing right now. The material offers useful, step-by-step guidance for any leader who wants to successfully navigate rapidly changing business environments from a place of calm presence. Susana shares her keen understanding and practical knowledge of how to create lasting change from the inside-out, which reliably impacts how we are able to show up more effectively in the organizations and communities we are leading. Her translation of Doug Silsbee's work is spot on, and incorporates presence and the awareness it offers in a seamless and engaging way.

Beatrice Hansen, Principal of Presence-Based Coaching, founded by the late Doug Silsbee, and author of *Presence-Based Coaching* and *Presence-Based Leadership*

Do you have a hunger to discover and express the leader within you in your job or family? *Insatiable Leaders* by Susana Martínez Denia gives you direct access to being a leader in any situation, nurturing six transformational skills.

Robert Hargrove, author of *Masterful Coaching*

Insatiable Leaders by Susana Martínez Denia is an invaluable resource for any leader committed to excellence and transformation. Drawing on her in-the-trenches experience with international business leaders, Susana explores the DNA of insatiable leaders – six key traits that drive significant impact. Her nuanced perspective on the double-edged nature of these traits provides a critical toolkit for navigating the complexities of leadership. This book is a must-read for leaders aiming to elevate their impact, foster a culture of continuous innovation, and stay ahead in a rapidly changing world.

Peter Hill, Counsel to Expat Executives and International Business Leaders and former Senior Director of Career Advancement at Hult International Business School

Insatiable leaders are the breed our world needs. But how do you become one? And if you already feel the passion to grow, how do you make it work for you instead of against you? I believe that true passion for progress emerges from a foundation of values amplified by mindful practice, openness to feedback and a growth mindset.

Insatiable Leaders is the book that will help you shape your approach to cultivating these by confronting you with the right questions at the right time. It's not a rule book. It's a thoughtful, kind and strong companion. The better to enjoy the journey!

Andrey Lipattsev, Partnership Development Manager at Google and Co-founder of The Tech Alliance Pod

Insatiable Leaders is a must-read for anyone looking to elevate their leadership skills and embrace a mindset of continuous improvement. What sets this book apart is its actionable advice and relatable anecdotes, which make the principles of insatiable leadership both accessible and compelling. Susana not only inspires readers but also equips them with the tools and mindset needed to drive their teams and organizations forward with steady determination.

Whether you are an experienced coach, a seasoned executive or an emerging leader, *Insatiable Leaders* will ignite your passion for growth and push you to surpass your limits. It's a powerful reminder that true leaders are never satisfied with the status quo: they are always hungry for more!

Valeria Bille, Organizational Psychologist and former Executive Director and Business Strategist at Goldman Sachs

In today's constantly changing environment, being a leader requires the best from all of us. Don't pass up the opportunity to read an inspiring and transformative leadership book. Susana Martínez Denia shares the essential factors for continuous learning, skill improvement and personal growth. This book not only guides you towards success in both your personal and professional life, but also inspires you to strive for excellence.

Fernando Campos, CEO DKV Spain

Susana is passionate about supporting individual leaders to be agents of transformation who can continuously adapt to the new challenges and opportunities that ongoing disruption presents.

Along with the type of leaders I write about in my own work, the leaders we'll increasingly need to affect this transformation are wired differently, think differently, challenge the way things have always been done and are driven to always improve their own leadership, those around them and the wider organization in which they choose to be.

If you're ready for a book that introduces strategies and a model for how leaders like this who are already in your organization can impact their environment by demonstrating, refining and evolving what she terms the six traits of 'insatiable leaders', then this serves as an invaluable guide.

Akin to FIRED leaders, if these leaders are seen and embraced for what they bring to organizations, they will become your greatest asset for navigating the ongoing uncertainty that disruption presents.

Paul McCarthy, Best-Selling Author of *The FIRED Leader: Reinventing the Future of Leadership*, Speaker and Thought Leader on the Future of Leadership

INSATIABLE LEADERS

Master your six transformative traits to fuel limitless growth

SUSANA MARTÍNEZ DENIA

First published in Great Britain by Practical Inspiration Publishing, 2024

© Susana Martínez Denia, 2024

The moral rights of the author have been asserted.

ISBN   9781788606226 (hbk)
        9781788606233 (pbk)
        9781788606257 (epub)
        9781788606240 (mobi)

Every effort has been made to trace copyright holders and to obtain their permission for the use of copyright material. The publisher apologizes for any errors or omissions and would be grateful if notified of any corrections that should be incorporated in future reprints or editions of this book.

Want to bulk-buy copies of this book for your team and colleagues? We can customize the content and co-brand *Insatiable Leaders* to suit your business's needs.

Please email info@practicalinspiration.com for more details.

To my Insatiable Clients:

Your essence, aspirations, restlessness and humanity transpire through each page of this book.

Thank you.

Contents

Preface xv

Introduction xviii

The DNA of an insatiable leader: six traits xviii

Why do we need insatiable leadership? xix

The cost of disconnected, limited and slowed-down leaders for
organizations xxii

The dark side of the traits xxiii

How to use this book xxv

Part I – Insatiable nature 1

1   Deconstructing insatiability: mapping insatiable
    drivers to the three dimensions of transformation 3

A critical cohort: beyond high-performers and high-potentials 4

What drives insatiable leaders? Insights from explorers, athletes and
time-benders 8

The three dimensions of transformation that insatiable leaders are
wired to master but are trapped in 15

The leadership box that caps growth and transformation 17

Fundamentals 21

Into the fishbowl: assessment and intention 22

2 The six traits in action: your superpower and your curse to lead transformation 23

Trait 1: Endlessly curious and unstoppable learners.......................... 24

Trait 2: Think big and question the limits..31

Trait 3: Raise the bar and standards of excellence 37

Trait 4: Multitalented, ultra-capable and overscheduled.......... 44

Trait 5: Self-reliant and determined..51

Trait 6: Sense of urgency to step into the future............................ 58

Channel your traits 65

Fundamentals 67

Into the fishbowl: challenge your traits 68

Part II – Insatiable elevation: a three-pillar model 69

3 Elevate your vision...73

A vision that pulls you: transform yourself and your organization......... 74

Strategy 1: Take a stand: at the intersection of your organizational and personal aspirations 78

Strategy 2: Stretch: pioneer visions, pioneer leaders 88

Strategy 3: Focus: an inward journey, a future declaration 95

Fundamentals 100

Into the fishbowl: draw and declare a pioneer vision that transforms you and your company... 101

4 Elevate your identity..103

Why do we need to change? (even if we are successful and ultra-capable).. 104

Step 1: Meet your identity and the box it traps you in 107

Step 2: Surface your identity 113

Step 3: Upgrade your identity 116

Step 4: Reinforce your new identity... 123

The 4Rs for your ongoing identity elevation 125

Fundamentals 128

Into the fishbowl: bring intentionality to your development.................. 130

5   Elevate your environment...131

Become a catalyst of the environment: the paradox to upgrade it 132

Strategy 1: Foster a team of A-players... 138

Strategy 2: Create units of excellence: high-performing teams and
micro-cultures 151

Strategy 3: Master the political chessboard 159

Fundamentals 172

Into the fishbowl: catalyse your environment in the next month 174

Part III – The two insatiable meta-abilities................ 175

6   Meta-abilities: tools for limitless growth.............. 177

The hallmark of insatiability: an ongoing growth journey 177

Meta-ability 1: Non-linear time management..179

Meta-ability 2: Presence 190

Fundamentals 197

Into the fishbowl: into your fishbowl challenge 198

Epilogue – One last dance: harness your insatiability ..199

Appendix A: Web-based resources 203

Appendix B: Further reading.. 205

About the author 207

Acknowledgements: my environment 209

Notes 211

Index...215

Insatiable

Adjective – In·sa·tia·ble /ɪnˈseɪʃəb(ə)/
Impossible to satisfy.

Insatiable Leader

An inquisitive, forward-thinking, bar raiser and multitalented leader with a dose of grit and restlessness to grow.

They're wired to envision endless possibilities to lead their businesses and others to new growth horizons despite obstacles.

Preface

The term 'insatiable' often carries a negative connotation, implying a craving, goal or desire that persists despite efforts to fulfil it, thereby leading to difficulty in achieving balance or perpetual dissatisfaction.

However, I cannot help but see that when harnessed, constructive dissatisfaction becomes the very engine that propels us, driving us to reach greater heights and explore new horizons.

It's the essence that has brought humankind forward.

It's the essence at the core of an Olympian athlete's spirit to give their best in their pursuit of excellence.

And it's the essence at the core of the leaders that relentlessly advance their organizations, inspire their teams to grow, drive change and make an impact in their industries.

Insatiable Leaders® is a leadership development initiative that emerged when I started to distil the essence of leaders I had coached who intrigued me by their approach to growth and their eagerness and intensity to experience it.

From our conversations, I distilled their drivers, fears and mindsets, and I identified six traits that marked them out and equipped them to be transformation agents in their organizations. They were avid learners, disruptors, bar raisers, multitalented, determined and with their minds in the future, eager to grasp it.

However, I realized how, ironically, these same traits that propelled them through growth thresholds played against them, capping their growth and the transformation they could lead and what they were after.

Their insatiable essence was a source of drive and fuel for growth, but also a source of frustrations, doubts and limitations that trapped these leaders in inefficiencies and exhaustion for elevating their results.

Grasping their experience of this duality helped me gain new insights about my own. Each leader revealed to me a part of who I was as I observed and distilled their essence; an aspiration that I craved, a trait that I had or a trap I was falling into that frustrated my growth journey.

In a dance between their stories and my own experience, my calling started to take shape. I committed and devoted myself to grasping this essence to turn it into a comprehensive leadership development framework to foster the advancement of critical leaders who seek to drive growth and transformation in organizations.

In this book, you will find insights and stories that evolve around the concept of 'insatiability': that feeling of hunger, a sense that there is more you could experience, change, contribute to or do, combined with an eagerness that propels you to explore it. An itch that, if not channelled, can hold you back in your growth.

The purpose of my book is to share my conclusions, strategies and leadership model, which are critical for leaders wired by these traits to channel these characteristics to the leaders' advantage to fuel growth and transformation.

My findings have emerged from my research, coaching and training sessions, and interviews with these leaders across countries, cultures and industries. Since 2017, I've been dedicated to finding and connecting with leaders in financial markets, consulting, AI or tech sectors; heads of divisions, partners or entrepreneurs that, regardless of their title, business unit, company or location, share one thing in common: their essence.

The insights I share in my book have been critical for their development and my own – I'm insatiable at heart. I've applied them to coach and train leaders in global corporations and I now seek to share them with other leaders. This book is for those who identify with aspects of these traits, lead someone who does or would like to gain fresh perspectives on their leadership and how these traits can foster their growth.

To enhance this, I've dedicated some chapters in the book to clients and leaders who have inspired me. Some of their names have been changed for privacy reasons. I've reported on their stories, adapted our conversations and shared with you sketches that I've drawn in sessions to illustrate leadership concepts that can help channel your eagerness to grow and fuel your transformation.

I believe that extraordinary leadership occurs when leaders discover what they're hungry for and use it as a driving force to take a stand, propel themselves into the future, overcome barriers and inspire those around them to do the same.

This is a provocative book to put you back in touch with yourself and the stand you take as a leader. It will guide you to explore, resolve and channel your inner hunger, ideas, aspirations and talents to create next-level meaningful results for a more inspiring, more transformative future.

Be insatiable,

Susana Martínez Denia
Executive Coach and Founder of Insatiable Leaders®

Introduction

The DNA of an insatiable leader: six traits

The concept of insatiable leaders hit me when I distilled the traits of clients that intrigued me for their innate sense of growth and the intensity, degree and speed at which they wanted to experience it.

I identified six traits that I repeatedly observed in these clients and leaders who achieved outstanding results.

1. They are **endlessly curious and unstoppable learners**, craving to learn more about the world and themselves.

2. They **think big and question the limits**, seeking to challenge the norm and make a difference.

3. They **raise the bar and standards of excellence**, for themselves and others.

4. They are **multitalented, ultra-capable and overscheduled**, committing and excelling in multiple challenges.

5. They are **self-reliant and determined**, and 'impossible' is banned from their vocabulary.

6. They have a **sense of urgency to step into the future**, being ten steps ahead of others, and ten steps behind where they would like to be.

As I distilled these traits, I realized how these leaders were hungry to grow and become a better version of who they were. These traits were their strategies to fuel their growth journey, so they would seek to leverage them incessantly to reach new growth thresholds.

They were insatiable.

They were eager to constantly surpass their limits; there will always be more knowledge that they'd be curious to access, new skills they'd seek to master, a bigger contribution they'd like to make and a new obstacle to overcome.

Why do we need insatiable leadership?

Leaders determine the role that companies play in this world.

Businesses and companies, regardless of their size, are the vehicle to produce the capacity for a larger contribution; but the leaders who drive them are the ones who set the course of an organization. The essence of a leader is then critical to define its direction, strategy and standards.

When that essence is insatiable, it equips leaders with curiosity, innovative capacity, drive for excellence, versatility, grit and agility to drive businesses forward and make a difference in a complex world of unexpected, accelerated and exponential global changes.

We live under a paradigm where change occurs unexpectedly, and it is convoluted by various factors such as social shifts, geopolitical challenges and fluctuations in energy and electricity industries. Moreover, technological breakthroughs further accelerate this complex and multi-layered environment.

These global events have an immediate impact on businesses and industries; on individuals and team morale; on company cultures and the way we work. Organizations that want to be ahead, prosper and play a part in this world need leaders to master the art of continuous change: identify it, create it, drive it and engage others in it.

That's why this world needs insatiable leaders. They're critical because:

- they are equipped to act as agents of transformation.
- they drive transformation continuously and expansively.

Agents of transformation across three dimensions

The six traits identified in this introduction give leaders an edge to understand, thrive and navigate this complex reality across three critical dimensions of transformation that I have also identified. These are:

i.   **Impact**: the relevance and competitiveness of strategies in a convoluted world.
ii. **Performance**: the level of excellence at which leaders and teams operate and generate results.
iii. **Momentum**: how quickly they achieve next-level results in a constantly evolving reality.

The traits help leaders drive transformation across each one of these dimensions:

- **Impact**: enable these leaders to gain an edge in identifying the evolving needs of industries and people, allowing them to shape new services or strategies to address them, make an impact and define a new norm.
- **Performance**: wire them to stretch themselves to operate at a higher level of performance and complexity in a multi-layered reality and inspire others and the organization to do the same.
- **Momentum**: provide them with the determination and agility to overcome the obstacles they encounter in the journey to gain momentum and be ahead in a constantly evolving world.

These leaders don't operate in the domain of what has been established; they are willing to operate in the domain of creativity, risk and uncertainty to bring the company and industries to new places.

Furthermore, their essence not only wires them to do this once but continuously.

Ongoing transformation: expansive leaders, expansive world

The hallmark of insatiability is expansiveness – a never-ending innate drive to grow.

The interesting point here is that by breaking through growth thresholds continually, these leaders expand in knowledge, relationships, ideas, talents, skills, experiences and strategies to be ahead.

This is important for organizations because as these leaders advance, they increase their capacity to play a bigger part in their area of business, environment and company, transferring the perks of their individual growth journeys into their system.

The more they expand in their own journeys driven by their insatiable essence to continually grow, the more of a ripple effect they can have in their organizations.

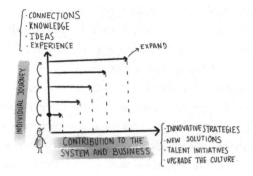

Leaders who continuously seek to grow and expand increase their capacity to promote continuous transformation under this complex and multi-layered paradigm we currently live in.

However, I observed how this transfer from individual perks into the business and system does not always happen fully. It can lack intention, focus and strategy, capping these leaders' potential to drive transformation at every stage of their growth journeys.

The cost of disconnected, limited and slowed-down leaders for organizations

Leaders marked out by the six insatiable traits do not always operate at the fullest capacity to drive the transformation that their DNA wires them to. Too often they're disconnected from their call, limited in their performance or slowed down by their system in their journeys.

This caps their advancement across the three critical dimensions of transformation in the following way:

- **Impact**: they are disconnected from their leadership call, not leveraging their ideas, knowledge and talents to lead impactful visions or projects that would put their companies ahead, showcase their expertise, maximize their potential and drive them internally.

- **Performance**: they find themselves limited in their performance as they navigate complex and challenging situations and increased demands, and they are exhausted and frustrated because their efforts or strategies seem inefficient and are not translating into elevated results. This is because they either hit a glass ceiling, constantly experience a gap between where they are now and where they would like to be, or they find it difficult to sustain themselves in complexity.
- **Momentum**: they face obstacles in the organizational system they operate in that block or slow down their advancement. Blockages arise from bureaucratic obstacles and internal politics within their organizations, where they experience stakeholders blocking change or the culture does not promote innovation and/ or agility. They're also slowed down by chaos or inefficiencies in execution and coordination or underperformance of their teams and their overloaded calendars.

It's in this paradigm of exponential change when leaders with these traits are most needed to make a dent, but they are trapped in a 'survival syndrome' – a short-term, future mentality that leaves little space for intentional, meaningful growth and transformation.

What's interesting is that this same essence that equips them to be game changers is what renders them ineffective.

The dark side of the traits

Ironically, the same traits that set these leaders apart as transformation agents can play against them; they act like a double-edged sword, both promoting and hindering their growth and capacity for transformation.

They do it in the following ways:

1. **Endlessly curious and unstoppable learners**: as extraordinary learners, they overexpose themselves to endless sources of information. Yet, the greater the options, the less satisfied and

confident they feel with their choices, and their knowledge does not always translate into robust initiatives that would put them and their companies ahead of the competition.

2. **Think big and question the limits**: they challenge the status quo and seek to cultivate their differences to stand out from the crowd. But when they hit the inevitable roadblocks to achieving something bigger, they question their vision, credibility or resources to achieve it.

3. **Raise the bar and standards of excellence**: they strive for mastery and the highest standards of excellence in everything they do. Yet, the closer they get to what they want, the further away they feel and the harder they are on themselves.

4. **Multitalented, ultra-capable and overscheduled**: they're known for being at 130% of their capacity, immersing themselves with excitement and competence in new challenges. But they risk investing energy in commitments that are not making a difference towards what they really want to achieve, making them feel drained or behind.

5. **Self-reliant and determined**: 'impossible' is banned from their vocabulary; they find the answers they need, and they overcome challenges with little or no help from others. But the higher they go, the more isolated they feel from the others around them, and fewer people are able to give them the inspiration, challenge and support they and their system need to transform.

6. **Sense of urgency to step into the future**: when they see a possibility, they want to take immediate action, and they wish those around them would follow their pace. Their mind is on the future, and they find it counterintuitive to slow down and make adjustments to their priorities, habits or environment to get closer to their ambitions quicker.

Each one of these traits can make these leaders ineffective across the three critical dimensions of transformation – limiting their impact, performance and momentum – thereby frustrating their growth journeys and capping the transformation they can drive.

To get out of this trap, these leaders need to relate differently to these traits and channel them to their service and advantage to support their growth. They need to harness the full potential of their ideas, knowledge, diverse talents and energy to fuel the transformation required under a complex and constantly changing reality.

That's why we need a new developmental framework to foster the growth of leaders with these traits.

That's why we need this book.

How to use this book

The purpose of this book is to empower leaders to channel the six traits to their advantage in the different stages of their growth journeys to fuel meaningful transformation and drive advancement and expansion in their areas of business, teams and organizations.

The most significant impact in driving this transformation can be made by intervening at the heart of the thought process of a critical leader, which in turn sets the direction and culture of a business, division or team. This book seeks exactly that.

Leaders who relate to the concept of insatiability and their traits, or who lead someone in their team who embraces these qualities, will find this book invaluable. Equally, it's for any inquisitive leader looking to boost their impact, performance and momentum or foster the six traits.

This book contains six chapters organized into three main parts to help you understand how the essence and traits of insatiability operate and how you can channel them to your ongoing individual and company advancement.

Part I explores the **insatiable nature**. First, it delves into the frustrations and drivers of insatiable leaders and the critical role they play in organizations to lead transformation across the three dimensions, and presents a map to foster their growth and development.

The focus then shifts to an exploration of each one of the six traits in detail and how they manifest in leaders' day-to-day situations. You will learn the dual nature of each trait and the shift you need to make to master their traps and fuel transformation.

Part II focuses on the **three-pillar model** to optimize leaders across the three dimensions of transformation by channelling their traits to their individual and company's advantage. Each one of these pillars is covered separately to share the strategies that create next-level results.

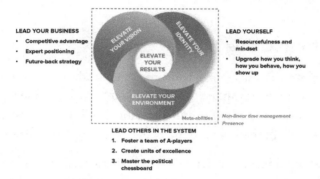

- In **elevate your vision**, you will discover the three strategies to craft a pioneering vision to provide the business you lead with a competitive edge, elevate your expert positioning and craft a future-back strategy to lead it.
- In **elevate your identity**, you will understand what limits you from producing higher results, and you will learn strategies to upgrade your mindset and behaviours to operate at higher levels of complexity, performance and excellence.
- In **elevate your environment**, you will explore the three strategies to help you achieve impactful results at scale: foster a team of A-players, create units of excellence with high-performing teams and micro-cultures and master the political chessboard.

Lastly, **Part III** delves into the two enablers to unlock infinite advancement and transformation – the two **insatiable meta-abilities**: non-linear time management and presence.

Throughout this book, you'll meet **11 leaders** – six women and five men – representing diverse nationalities and industries, whose stories and conversations have inspired me to illustrate the concepts that I aim to share with you.

In each chapter, you'll find **sketches** that I've drawn in coaching conversations and group training. Through visual thinking, I externalise and make more explicit internal thinking processes and complex ideas that have come up in conversations intended to foster leadership development.

At the end of each chapter, you'll find two sections: '**Fundamentals**', which summarizes the key ideas of each chapter, and '**Into the fishbowl**'.

'Into the fishbowl' is an analogy I use to refer to the space of self-reflection leaders need to create out of their hectic rhythms and day-to-day activities to gain new perspectives and generate new leadership insights. Leaders enhance those insights when they distance themselves from the system they lead – from their business, teams, clients, peers and management – and can look at it from a distance with a new lens. The fishbowl is that space from where they can look at it strategically.

In the 'Into the fishbowl' section at the end of each chapter, you'll find questions designed to elevate your strategic insights into how to lead your business, yourself and others in new ways to drive elevated results and transformation.

Let's dive in!

Part I
Insatiable
nature

This part delves into analysing the insatiable nature, how insatiable leaders are wired, and how their essence determines the growth and transformation they can drive in organizations.

Part I is all about the discovery. First, by laying the groundwork and dissecting the essence of insatiability and its impact on organizational transformation. Later, by venturing further into the reality of the six traits and uncovering how they can be both a superpower and a curse for growth along with strategies to channel them to propel advancement.

Chapter 1

Deconstructing insatiability: mapping insatiable drivers to the three dimensions of transformation

This chapter peels away the layers of insatiability to understand how it functions and maps it onto leadership foundations to help companies and leaders advance in their growth and transformation.

By the end of this chapter, you'll understand:

- how these leaders experience growth in comparison to high-performers and high-potentials.
- the three dimensions that insatiable leaders seek to master which, in turn, reveal the three dimensions for transformation in companies.
- how each trait equips leaders to master and grow in each dimension.
- the leadership box that traps them and caps their growth.

A critical cohort: beyond high-performers and high-potentials

'Once we accept our limits, we go beyond them.'
Albert Einstein

To Vanisha

Vanisha was one of the first leaders I came across in my journey whose essence I wanted to grasp. I wanted to understand how it functioned and made her experience growth, how it aimed to maximize her potential and the contribution she could make in her organization.

She was the Chief Operating Officer of support services at a global brokerage firm, responsible for driving change across the organization. She instilled a weather-beaten spirit, which she had nurtured and strengthened by progressing through aspirations and challenges in her journey.

A disruptor at the core, she would constantly brainstorm improvements for her organization, seeking to challenge the norm and mobilize other players in this change, even if this did not always happen to the standards and speed that she envisioned, despite her eagerness.

She was used to juggling multiple hats, considering the different back office departments she needed to interact with, for example, legal, client onboarding and tech. This equipped her to thrive in a multidisciplinary reality with increasing and complex demands.

As I observed her, I couldn't help but notice how her essence matched the six traits that I had started to map from a few other leaders who, like her, had got my attention.

These leaders demonstrate these characteristics:

1. Endlessly curious and unstoppable learners.
2. Think big and question the limits.
3. Raise the bar and standards of excellence.
4. Multitalented, ultra-capable and overscheduled.
5. Self-reliant and determined.
6. Have a sense of urgency to step into the future.

Vanisha would leverage that blend of inquisitiveness, disruption, versatility, grit and eagerness to grow, to propel both her own progress and that of her colleagues, actively seeking the transformation of her organization.

Her attitudes, attributes and potential had put her into a pool most organizations define as 'high-performer' and 'high-potential'; those that are identified as 'key talent' to be nurtured for future promotion to become the organization's leaders who will continue to drive organizational performance and advancement.

However, I could not help but notice that there was a distinctive touch in her approach to advancement in her career and within the organization. This manifested in the degree to which she wanted to drive growth, the level at which she wanted to implement it, the speed at which she wanted it to happen and the frequency at which she wanted it to take place.

The six traits were the drivers that explained Vanisha's growth experience. However, the growth experience for insatiable leaders can be different to the growth experience that high-performers and high-potentials encounter.

High-performers vs high-potentials vs insatiable leaders

There are distinct characteristics of high-performers, high-potentials and insatiable leaders:

- **High-performers** (or high-achievers) achieve outstanding results consistently, exceeding expectations of what their role requires.
- **High-potentials**, while achieving superior levels of performance, exhibit behaviours and attitudes that reflect their companies' culture and values in an exemplary manner and have the capacity to grow and rise quickly to more critical positions within the organization and succeed in them.[1] This is because they align with what's required by the organizational framework under which they operate.
- **Insatiable leaders** encompass the qualities of both high-performers and high-potentials, equipped and driven to stand out in their roles or organizational frameworks. However, they actively seek to challenge these organizational frameworks and redefine new ones that are more relevant and competitive to the circumstances of the market, their industries and their people.

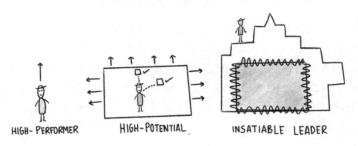

HIGH-PERFORMER   HIGH-POTENTIAL   INSATIABLE LEADER

Insatiable leaders question the status quo and how things operate – in the culture, strategy or team. They constantly seek to push the limits to reach the next level and redefine them to conceive new ways to serve customers, advance the industry, upgrade the culture and engage their people.

In the spectrum and universe of leaders who seek transformation, and are equipped to lead growth and transformation, the six traits distinguish insatiable leaders, shaping their growth experience in unique ways.

They leverage these traits as strategies to fuel advancement and explore new spaces shaped by a constantly evolving and complex reality. They stretch their people, systems and culture to optimize their potential within these new spaces and be ahead in them.

But as they seek to reshape the limits in their journey, they also experience unique frustrations that hold the clue to understanding their essence.

Surfacing frustrations reveals the clues to map the characteristics of insatiability

Vanisha often felt that she could contribute and achieve more – and quicker.

The frustrations that her and other leaders experience fall under three categories relating to the type of objectives they pursue, their capacity to achieve them and/or the blockages they find in the system that they lead:

- They consider they are not maximizing their knowledge, talent and ideas in their growth journeys.
- Their efforts or strategies are not translating into the results they envision, despite their commitment and perseverance.
- They are held back from being ahead in a constantly evolving reality and they are frustrated because their system – procedures, team, peers and management – doesn't match the pulse of the change that they consider required for their organizations to be ahead.

To overcome some of these barriers, Vanisha needed to understand more about how she inherently operated. Her traits gave her a unique nuance in her approach to growth and she needed to understand what she wanted to achieve, how her qualities contributed to her advancement and what was holding her back from an elevated growth experience and the bigger contribution that she envisioned.

Mapping these elements into a framework will enable leaders with these traits to gain new insights into how they grow to foster their advancement and maximize their contribution to their organizations.

What drives insatiable leaders? Insights from explorers, athletes and time-benders

What was Vanisha hungry for? And what were the limits she sought to challenge and surpass?

Researching humankind, it became apparent that the essence of insatiability, of the search for more, had always been present in our history, propelling us to evolve and surpass our limits. This realization set me on a path to further explore real-world examples where insatiability manifested, aiming to grasp how the essence and traits characterizing these leaders were displayed in a wider context.

Insights from human evolution, athletes and physicists helped me identify the patterns of what makes insatiable leaders hungry. I started to find connections between these discoveries and my conversations with insatiable leaders to map out the three dimensions to guide these leaders and companies in their growth.

The story of human evolution: the power of ideas and observation to advance the world further

Insatiable leaders, in fact, have been around as long as sapiens.

In his book *Sapiens*, Yuval Noah Harari explains the three revolutions that shaped human history and enabled humans to spread, thrive and conquer the world:

    i.   The **Cognitive Revolution** gave sapiens a new edge with the gift of language, helping create a common understanding and share stories (myths) about things that exist only in our imagination.

ii. The **Agricultural Revolution** led to exponential population growth and pushed humanity to develop laws, money and systems to operate, cooperate and regulate the population and organize it at scale.

iii. The **Scientific Revolution** was when humans shifted to a worldview where they realized they could learn about the world and improve it from scientific principles of exploration, experimentation and observation. This scientific approach pushed humans to look for answers to make substantial leaps and progress, for example, in areas such as medicine, physics and global commerce.

The three revolutions centre around the principle that sapiens, our race of humans, are mythmakers who connect and create around ideas that exist in their imagination. And how shared ideas that live in humans' imagination prompted them to consider new visions and possibilities to explore, leading to change and advancement.

Harari's reconstruction of human evolution, specifically the Scientific Revolution, gave me insight into how the power of ideas, inquisitiveness and observation are engines of transformation, advancement and improvement in our world. It's what has inspired leaders in humankind to evolve, and what's required by leaders who want to play a part in advancing this world.

But what does it mean, 'advancing the world'?

For example, the Magellan-Elcano expedition, the first circumnavigation of the globe, took place during the Scientific Revolution.[2]

The Portuguese explorer Ferdinand Magellan set sail from Seville, Spain, in 1519, prompted by the search for alternative spices in Asia that could not be cultivated in Europe. The expedition culminated three years later with the Spaniard Juan Sebastián Elcano returning in the only one of the five vessels that initially departed, having successfully opened up a new world trade route. This expedition established the foundations for global commerce for the first time and disrupted the way commerce was done then.

These explorers did not just walk by history; they made it. They advanced humanity by observing how to improve the world around them. It's that process of curiosity, observation and ideation that brought the world further on; the same process required by organizations who want to drive progress and make a difference in their industries and with their clients. It's that same process, the one leaders who want to catalyse progress and drive impact need to engage in.

That's what Vanisha was after. She was wired like an explorer who wanted to bring the world further on and channel her ideas, knowledge and expertise to challenge the norm with new solutions, strategies and products to advance her organization and make a difference.

To plant the seed to drive progress, Vanisha leveraged two traits: her curiosity and learning capacity to gather more knowledge about the world, and her disruptor mentality to challenge the status quo, prompting her to think creatively and push the boundaries to shape impactful initiatives.

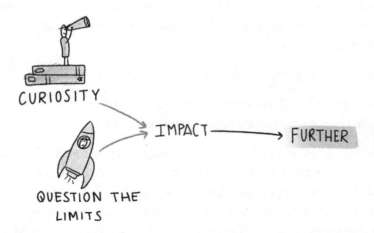

CURIOSITY

IMPACT ⟶ FURTHER

QUESTION THE LIMITS

However, the limits Vanisha wanted to challenge were not only the norm and status quo but also her own limits.

Sports: at the edge of excellence and constant improvement to reach higher

The original Olympic motto was 'Citius, Altius, Fortius', which was proposed by Pierre de Coubertin, the founder of the modern Olympic Games, and officially adopted in 1894. It means 'Faster, Higher, Stronger' and it symbolizes the pursuit of excellence and constant individual and collective improvement by striving to give one's best.[3]

It expresses the aspirations of the Olympic Movement not only in its athletic and technical sense, but also for everyone from an educational perspective.[4] It encapsulates the idea of stretching one's limits to grow and achieve elevated results.

It encapsulates the essence of insatiability.

It's that essence that transpires in elite athletes and players who constantly seek to elevate their performance and excellence, aiming to become their best version and inspire others to do the same.

It's that essence that is required in companies that seek to stand out.

Companies and their products and services stand out when leaders raise the bar and create an entirely new standard of measurement for themselves and others to perform to.

When leaders relentlessly seek new strategies for their teams through adversity, like football squads scoring three goals in the final minutes to reverse a match's outcome. When they strive for mastery in a diverse landscape, like tennis players adapting to conquer different court surfaces. When they're committed to sustaining excellence, paralleling golfers striving for perfection with every shot during their four-hour rounds.

Insatiable leaders are driven to repeatedly operate at higher levels of performance across multiple disciplines and challenges, and there are two traits that equip them for this: raising the bar and standards of excellence and being multitalented and ultra-capable.

Vanisha demonstrated these two traits, as she raised the bar to enhance her performance and fostered continuous improvement and as she sought to cultivate her multiple talents to be equipped to operate and excel in a complex and multidimensional reality.

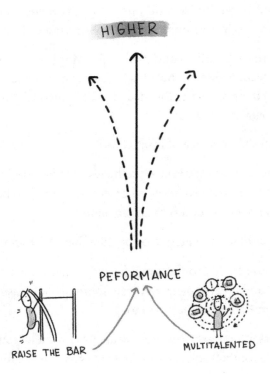

In her growth journey, Vanisha wanted to defy the limit of the status quo (impact) and her own limits (performance), but there was still one other limit that Vanisha wanted to defy. Another dimension that would give sense to the impact and performance she wanted to drive. The dimension that is the basis of Einstein's Theory of Relativity: *Time*.

The third dimension in the insatiable cosmos: bending time to go faster

In the Special Theory of Relativity, Einstein determined that time is relative – in other words, the rate at which you experience time depends on your frame of reference.[5]

Insatiable leaders are visionaries and forward-thinking leaders who, in fact, operate simultaneously in two frames of reference.

One is in their present, the status quo, framed by their current levels of growth, impact and performance and where their team, peers and company are. The other is their future, which represents an expansive universe of growth possibilities and is framed by what they would like to achieve and the new challenges they would like to pursue.

Their minds are on the future frame, excited about what could be possible for the growth they can experience, the impact they can drive and the performance they can reach. And they seek to bend time to bridge this gap between the present and the future they envision.

However, this can result in a tricky task for two reasons:

- From one side, the future they envision keeps moving further away from the present, as their aspirations increase and the world keeps constantly changing, pulling them into new spaces that reveal new possibilities to explore and challenges for them to grasp.
- On the other side, their present frame does not move as fast as they would like. This is because they operate under a complex system with diverse people, alongside intricate divisions, governance structures, cultural nuances and procedural frameworks, which don't always move swiftly and don't follow pace with their eagerness and increasing aspirations.

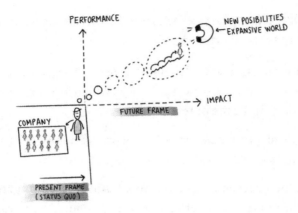

To bend time and catch up with their future vision, they need to gain momentum, driving the entire system forward with them to overcome obstacles and bridge the distance between these two frames that seem to be always moving further apart from each other.

Like time was the dimension that added a new level of understanding of how we are in the cosmos, together with understanding of length, width and height, it's also the dimension that complements the other two dimensions of impact and performance to understand how insatiable leaders operate in the insatiable cosmos.

Insatiable leaders don't measure their growth in an absolute manner. They do it relative to time and how fast they achieve the impact they want to drive and the performance they want to reach in a constantly evolving world.

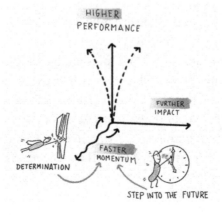

To be ahead, Vanisha would tap into her sense of urgency to step into the future, seeking to inject her energy and velocity to gain momentum. She would also rely on her self-reliance and determination to embrace change and challenges, remaining resilient in overcoming obstacles, rather than allowing them to impede or slow down her progress.

~

Like Vanisha, many other leaders marked out by the six traits leveraged them to go further, higher and faster.[6]

Insatiable leaders experience growth as explorers, athletes and time-benders.

They seek to drive more impact, achieve higher levels of performance and gain momentum. And it's exactly progression on these dimensions that would give organizations an edge in this paradigm of unexpected, accelerated and exponential change.

The three dimensions of transformation that insatiable leaders are wired to master but are trapped in

To play a part in this complex world and be ahead, companies need to master these three dimensions of impact, performance and momentum and optimize leaders in them:

- **Impact**: in a world of increasing challenges and exponential change, companies need innovative leaders who observe market trends; leaders who are committed to making a difference by addressing industry and customer needs through ground-breaking solutions such as new services, products or strategies.
- **Performance**: companies need leaders who are committed to stretching their abilities and mindsets to thrive under this challenging paradigm, who seek to master and operate in

a multidisciplinary reality to produce elevated results in a more complex world and inspire others to do the same.

- **Momentum**: companies need visionary leaders and time-benders who seek to be ahead in a constantly evolving world, with the capacity to absorb change fatigue, seeking to put the system in motion and bridge the gap between where they are now and where they want to be in the future, to put their companies ahead.

These three dimensions need to coexist. If any of them are compromised, then you'll hinder your competitiveness. *Omitting the impact* means initiatives and visions won't drive progress for your clients and industry. *Lowering the standards of performance and versatility* means the market will rule you out at the level at which you and your people operate. *Disregarding momentum* means you'll run behind the pulse of the market and the world.

Companies have an edge if they have leaders who are wired to thrive in these dimensions or seek to optimize leaders to progress in them.

Insatiable leaders could be strong candidates to set the motion for growth and advancement in each one of the three dimensions. However, while the six traits are powerful catalysts for transformation, Vanisha and other leaders wired by these traits don't experience the progression they envision in their advancement, and they don't drive the transformation that their traits wire them to.

In fact, in their day-to-day activities as leaders, they can be disconnected from their leadership calling, they don't always thrive in new domains of increased complexity and excellence, and they succumb to a system that blocks agility and transformation at scale.

While these traits can fuel their advancement in these three dimensions, they also restrict these leaders' growth simultaneously across each one of them:

- **Impact**: they are not maximizing their knowledge, expertise and talents to craft and lead impactful initiatives for their company that would put their company ahead and position them as experts to lead them.

- **Performance**: their eagerness to increase performance and efforts does not always translate into elevated results in the new spaces they would like to operate in, leading to exhaustion and frustration.

- **Momentum**: eager to gain momentum, leaders face obstacles in their environments such as misalignment, resistance to change and outdated procedures, and mindsets or culture that hinder progress. These barriers not only slow them down but also impede impactful transformation at scale that prevent them from engaging people in their system to change and achieve the necessary agility to drive their companies forward.

But why is this happening?

Why are insatiable leaders with such capacity to excel and drive transformation across these dimensions capped simultaneously on each one of them?

This is because their approach to leveraging each trait is ineffective for driving the results they want to achieve, and these traits trap insatiable leaders in a box.

The leadership box that caps growth and transformation

Robert Hargrove, founder of Masterful Coaching, has been an Executive Coach to presidential appointees, Fortune CEOs and Silicon Valley founders. Coaching top leaders that are at the highest levels, he shares how at any moment in our journeys, regardless of the levels of growth we have experienced, we are operating as if we were in a box that limits the results we create.[7]

This box is defined by your master programmes, which shape your understanding of the world, others and yourself, and limit and define how you perceive and respond to situations.

These programmes are shaped by and result in:

- perceptions and interpretations of a specific situation.
- winning strategies – ways of operating that have proven to be helpful in achieving your objectives up until now and getting to a predetermined level of success.
- practices and engrained ways of behaving and responding to situations.
- horizon of possibilities, which is what you perceive to be possible.

Inside this box, it's impossible to create new results different to the ones you've been used to creating.

To create higher results, you need to move beyond the limits of your current box. And for this, you need to understand the functioning of the master programmes that trap you in such box and challenge them to break out of it.

The insatiable box

These master programmes depend on your personal history, background and context. This means that they vary from one leader to another depending on the uniqueness of their journeys, and consequently, the conditioning that keeps each leader in their box is unique to them.

However, what's interesting is that leaders marked out by the six traits engage in recurrent patterns, ways of perceiving situations and default behaviours that can limit their development.

The traits are what keeps them in a box, capping their growth and the transformation they can lead and frustrating their aspirations to maximize their potential across the dimensions of impact, performance and momentum they so much want to master. And in turn, their companies are limited in the three dimensions where they need to thrive and play a part in this world.

This implies that, at any moment of the journey, if they try to make strides in each one of these dimensions, their traits trap them in a box.

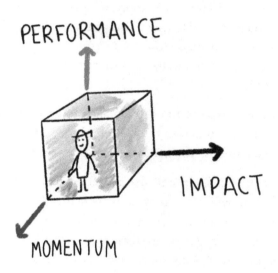

It's not possible inside that box to foster leaders who will make quantum leaps in the impact they can have, the performance standards at which they operate and the momentum they generate.

To grow to the next level in each dimension, you first need to understand how to break out of your box. For this, you need to understand the developmental edges of your traits and challenge them to consider new possibilities outside your box that you cannot see because the traits trap you there.

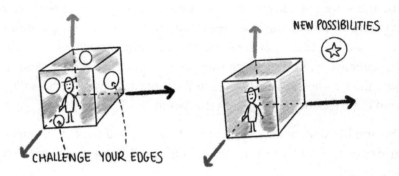

This means that to lead transformation and growth across these three dimensions, you first need to transform yourself. This is what we will explore in the next chapter. How does each one of these traits trap you, and how do you need to harness them to fuel your growth and transformation?

In Part II, we will explore the three-pillar model to optimize your growth and leadership across these three dimensions, once you've gained an edge into how you need to channel these traits.

At the end of this chapter, and the subsequent ones, the 'Into the fishbowl' section will provide you with self-reflection questions intended for you to break out of your box by either challenging your developmental edges or stretching your thinking to consider new possibilities. And with those insights, increase your impact, performance and momentum.

Fundamentals

- Insatiable leaders are a **leadership cohort** that operates in the domain of ongoing transformation. They need to understand how they're wired and how their traits shape their unique growth experience to maximize their potential and contribution to their personal advancement and organizational development.

- They operate as explorers, athletes and time-benders, seeking to go further, higher and faster by driving **impact**, increasing **performance** and gaining **momentum**.

- Their six traits equip them to progress on these three dimensions that are critical for organizations to be ahead in the domain of transformation. However, these qualities also cap their growth simultaneously on each dimension, trapping them in a **box**.

- Inside this box it is impossible to make quantum leaps and create new results, and to break out of it insatiable leaders need to understand how their essence operates to optimize their leadership and create next-level results.

Into the fishbowl: assessment and intention

 I invite you to assess your level of growth across the three dimensions and use your insights to set an intention to tackle and to have in mind as you read the book.

1. What has your **impact** been the past year? Why was it not higher? Why was it not lower? (The difference you've made in your business, industry and for your clients.)

2. What has your **individual performance** been the past year? Why was it not higher? Why was it not lower?

3. What has your **team performance** been the past year? Why was it not higher? Why was it not lower?

4. What has your **peer group performance** been the past year? Why was it not higher? Why was it not lower?

5. What are **two questions** that you would like to have answered from reading this book to help you elevate your impact, performance and/or momentum?

Chapter 2

The six traits in action: your superpower and your curse to lead transformation

These six traits can help insatiable leaders grow in three dimensions – impact, performance and momentum – but they can also limit them. This chapter explains this dual nature in action and how to harness each trait.

By the end of this chapter, you'll understand:

- how each trait fuels and limits individual and company growth, operating as a double-edged sword.
- the trap leaders fall into that perpetuates the inefficiencies of each trait.
- the shift that leaders need to make to channel each trait to fuel transformation.

I've dedicated each trait to a client who exemplifies its essence and has inspired me to write about it. For each of them, you will find a mix of dialogues and explanations; they are not exactly how our conversations evolved, but I've adapted them to illustrate the trait in action and the shift they needed to make.

At the end of the chapter, you'll find the story of how each client made the shift with each trait and how this impacted their leadership. We'll delve into the strategies that contributed to such shifts in detail in Part II – the insatiable elevation model.

Trait 1: Endlessly curious and unstoppable learners

As an extraordinary learner, you overexpose yourself to endless sources of information.

Yet, that knowledge does not always translate into robust initiatives that would put you and your company ahead of the competition and drive impact. And the greater the options, the less satisfied and confident you feel with your choices about what to do, lead and execute.

To...
The Ideators
The Seekers
The Eternal Students

To Laura

Laura was a Global Manager of Ad Operations at Play Station. She was constantly hungry for new knowledge and intellectual stimulation, forever finding books, podcasts, inspiring conversations and courses to develop herself, challenge her thinking and open her mind to new possibilities.

She was seeking to remain relevant in a constantly evolving world and her mind and habits were designed to absorb and integrate new information and knowledge. But she was overexposing herself to inputs, creating a non-stop cycle of stimulation and possibilities.

She thought she'd be satisfied by absorbing more and more ideas from the outside world when, in reality, she was craving to express her own ideas and be recognized as a thought leader in tech.

For this, she didn't need more knowledge or inspiration from the outside world; she needed focus to frame her ideas and the courage to own them. And she would not achieve this by looking outside to the next thing to learn but by looking within herself.

A double-edged sword: your knowledge does not translate into impact

"What are you after, Laura, book after book, podcast after podcast, course after course?" I asked, recognizing in her my own eagerness to learn and search for new perspectives to enrich my mind and life.

"I want to find that extra strategy that would give me an edge in the tech industry, raise my profile and help me stand out."

She embraced that desire to constantly be exposed to new trends, books, courses and networks that had always motivated me to explore and drove me further in my journey. There's one quote by Ken Robinson, authority on creativity and human potential, that captured this essence: 'Curiosity is the engine of achievement.'[1]

Inquisitive leaders who are unstoppable learners have the potential to shape new ideas to foster innovation, consider new solutions to provide their companies with a competitive edge and position them as an authority and expert. But in Laura, this potential was not translating into advancement for herself or her company.

"Laura," I said, "I see you feeding your mind with new knowledge, aspirations and possibilities. However, I don't see all that translating into the difference you want to make and that you can make. You said you wanted to stand out, but I don't see you taking a stand."

Her face lit up. "What do you mean by taking a stand?" she queried.

"It's your leadership cause, what you care about to advance towards in your company and industry. It's the case of transformation that would make you channel your knowledge, ideas and curiosity to shape it and mobilize resources – people, budget, technology – to bring it to life."

To find it, define it and craft it, Laura needed to look at the knowledge and the information she acquired through a new lens; not with the lens to learn and absorb more information, but with the lens to reframe it strategically to drive impact.

There are two lenses from which to consider curiosity and your capacity to learn:

- The **outside-in lens**, through which you absorb information from the outside world and develop knowledge.
- The **inside-out lens**, through which you engage in inner self-reflection to relate strategically with that knowledge and intentionally drive impact and advancement.

The outside-in lens drives you to absorb information and experiences from different sources such as books, podcasts, courses, events or conversations to expand your knowledge.

If you are inquisitive and an unstoppable learner, the consequence of this can be that the more you learn, the hungrier you are for more and new knowledge. This prompts you to absorb new and more information to quench that thirst, engaging in a pattern of constant learning without always impactfully applying that knowledge.

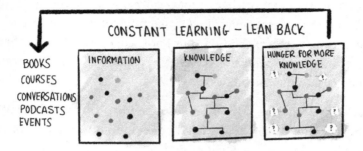

With the outside-in lens, as you engage in constant learning, you risk *leaning back* from the world, and you don't always put your knowledge at the service of your company and industry to make a difference.

To action this shift, you need to develop an inside-out lens to learning that focuses on driving innovation and impact.

For this, you need to relate your knowledge differently and strategically, as the image below illustrates.

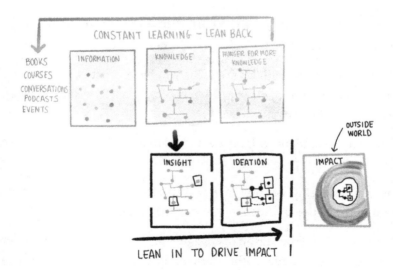

Figure adapted from Gapingvoid – Culture Design group.
Data Information Knowledge Insight Wisdom Impact

Considering your knowledge strategically involves engaging in introspection to generate new *insights* that might not be immediately apparent from merely expanding your knowledge base. You can then turn these new perspectives you've gained into *ideas* as you start seeing patterns and possibilities.

The ideation process is critical because the ideas that you generate can translate into initiatives, strategies or solutions to implement in the outside world, outside of your mind, to drive tangible impact.

Engaging in learning through the inside-out lens is critical to making a difference because the higher the quality of those insights, the more powerful and relevant the ideas and initiatives you'll bring into the world.

However, operating with an outside-in lens is not always obvious for leaders who, like Laura, gravitate naturally towards learning. Learning and expanding knowledge can become a comfort zone, and this is a trap that prevents driving impact.

The trap: learning and your mind have become your comfort zone

"So, tell me, Laura, with all the ideas you have, what else is missing for you to take a stand, make a difference and lead?" I asked, knowing that it was not more knowledge.

"I don't feel confident with my own ideas to bring them forward," she confessed.

She was wagering on how a new diploma and more knowledge would lead to the confidence that needed to come from within.

Laura hid behind the reason of engaging in constant learning in order to build her legitimacy. Other leaders do this to be up to date in a constantly changing world or a mere drive for knowledge.

Regardless of their explanation, leaders can trap themselves by engaging in the pattern of constant learning without impactful application of their knowledge, justifying this by saying they're growing because they're learning. Some of them can go a step further and start ideating, reorganizing their knowledge into business ideas, but their knowledge and ideas don't leave their minds.

Leadership is a game that happens in the outside world, where powerful ideas are at the core of business visions and strategies that make a difference and position leaders who drive them forward as experts in their fields.

But for this, leaders need to leave their comfort zone of learning or even ideating. Their ideas need to leave their minds.

This means that your knowledge needs to be strategically explored and restructured into powerful ideas that in turn are challenged, channelled and actioned towards producing impactful results that make a difference and position you as an authority.

This requires a different type of curiosity: you need to look within.

The shift: curiosity towards yourself

Your ideas shaped into strategies, products or services are your intellectual property (IP).

What would give you and your company an edge in business is curating and commercializing your IP. Powerful ideas, not knowledge, is what puts you and your company ahead.

To exploit your IP, you need to know yourself and nurture your curiosity from the inside out.

This lens prompts you to look inwards to understand your drivers and explore your knowledge and experiences strategically. It enables you to challenge and nurture your ideas and explore their business potential. When you do this, you can then channel and reframe your knowledge into robust initiatives that would advance your company and elevate your expert positioning.

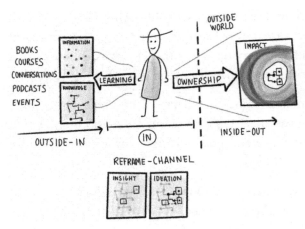

It's by shifting the focus *IN* (inwards) that you can explore how you connect with your knowledge to generate new insights and take ownership of your ideas. The self-reflection questions that you'll find in Part II are designed strategically to guide you in this.

It was when Laura turned the focus *IN* that she transformed how she assessed her legitimacy.

The validation of her credibility she once sought externally by acquiring new knowledge was now internally sourced. She realized that, with the knowledge and insights she had already gained, she could elevate her profile and advance her business unit. She surfaced and identified untapped business opportunities and key operational inefficiencies that, if addressed, would give her and her division an edge. As she engaged in strategic self-reflection, she developed her own views and business criteria, and gained confidence in her judgements as she saw how her ideas could make an impact in her team and company.

She took a stand for what she cared about to make strides in her career. She crafted a vision and strategy that got her promoted to lead the Ad Operations department globally. In parallel, she created her own coaching project to coach women in tech, elevating her expert positioning in this industry.

Once you've channelled your ideas and you're ready to lead them in the outside world, you'll need to overcome the barriers you'll find on the journey. And challenging the next trait holds the clue to succeed in this.

Trait 2: Think big and question the limits

You challenge the status quo and search to cultivate your difference to stand out from the crowd.

But when you hit the inevitable roadblocks of achieving something bigger, you blame the environment and question your vision, your credibility or the resources to make it happen.

To...
The Disruptors
The Pioneers
The Visionaries

To Mariví

Mariví had just been promoted to Head of the Eurodrone Programme Quality in Airbus when we met. Her commitment and enthusiasm to grow astonished her clients and made her teams and the projects she worked on shine. But she was hungry to make a bigger difference in her company and play a new game.

She saw the potential that technology offered to address gaps in the market to put her company ahead and the impact her division could have if they were more agile. She observed how inefficient ways of operating were leaving her company out of the game, and jokingly shared how she envisioned turning her division into a Ferrari to gain an edge.

She saw possibilities to do things differently in her company. In fact, she saw impossibilities. She lived already in that world that she could not grasp but could visualize and she was determined to bring peers and stakeholders on board.

But this, of course, was not that easy.

Her organizational system would resist change, and she started to face obstacles and question herself. She would pull back from transformation into projects she knew she would thrive in, depriving her company, teams and clients of the transformation she envisioned; what her people needed and what she craved.

A double-edged sword: you question the status quo but you question yourself

"So, tell me, Marivi, what's holding you back from building and driving that Ferrari you told me about?"

She gave a hint of a smile amid her frustration and disappointment. "It is not that straightforward to change things in this company. And I even wonder whether this is what I want to do..."

As I listened to her questioning, it was my turn to smile, recognizing that self-sabotage I knew well – that voice, that questioning, those doubts that kicked in when I aimed to set myself high aspirations.

What brings companies to new places is the capacity of a leader to question the status quo, challenge how things are done and take a stand that they can be done differently, thereby shaping and driving visions that align with what the world, clients or the company need.

As Oscar Wilde said: 'The world is made by the signs of the dreamers.'

That capacity to question is what drives change and innovation. But it can play against leaders as they face obstacles and their environment resists change.

Marivi's mind was designed to question the status quo in her company and look for gaps and possibilities of what could be done differently. But in the same way she questioned the outside world, she also questioned her vision, her resources, her capacities, her purpose or what can be possible in the system she operated in. Her mind was designed to look for gaps in her abilities and resources to drive her big vision and aspirations further.

As Mariví aimed to build her Ferrari and lead change in her organization, her external and internal systems responded to this, triggering doubts about herself and surfacing others' agendas and governance structures in her organization that blocked her progress.

I noticed her discouragement and frustration as she started to speak about culture, ego games, politics, career crisis, not being ready and her self-diagnosis of imposter syndrome.

Engaging in this narrative about obstacles had taken her focus away from her vision of transformation. In disconnecting from it, she inadvertently perpetuated the status quo she so much wanted to change.

The trap: you focus on the obstacles, play a smaller game and perpetuate the status quo

When leaders start fixating on obstacles, they shift their focus away from their vision to what's blocking their progress.

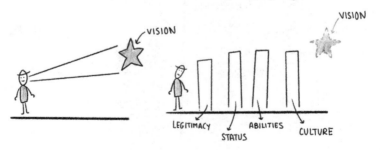

When this happens, their leadership case is no longer about their vision for transformation they want to drive forward, rather it is about the obstacles they need to face and whether they're capable or not to face them. This is the trap Mariví had fallen into.

What she was overlooking is that these resistances were a by-product of dreaming big and aiming for an ambitious vision of transformation.

"Mariví, the bigger the game you want to play, the bigger the resistances you'll face – the more people will resist change and the more your credibility will be at stake to drive that vision to success. It's like physics," I joked, speaking to her engineer soul.

"Ok, but I still need to overcome these obstacles."

"Of course, but you're so fixated upon them that they have made you lose perspective of where you're going and the big game you wanted to play. As a result, you have reduced your vision to 'just' overcoming these obstacles. If managing politics or proving your competency is what you aim for, then that's a very uninspiring vision for your organization and your own growth."

Making the journey about obstacles had led Mariví to play a smaller game.

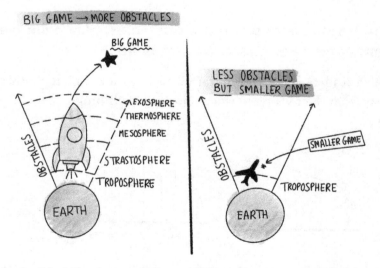

I doubt Mariví's team at Airbus will hire me as an aircraft designer with this drawing, but it illustrates what, unfortunately, I see many leaders do.

As leaders face the inevitable obstacles of achieving something bigger, they can be trapped in hustling through the journey, firefighting and hitting walls. Gradually, they leave their big ambitions behind, and they reduce their vision to a level where they believe they can manage or have fewer and less demanding obstacles.

While a smaller game might involve fewer obstacles to face, it doesn't spark leaders and doesn't ignite transformation, thereby perpetuating the status quo. In these situations, leaders disconnect from driving transformation and their leadership stand, when it's precisely what their companies need to progress and what they need to be pulled through obstacles.

"Mariví, if you buy into the story of culture, ego or politics, you're making this about others. If you make this about your credibility, you're making it about you. I see you either making a case about yourself, others or any obstacle, but you're no longer making a case about transformation and not betting on something you care about. And this is precisely what will take you to the other side of obstacles: your vision."

Ironically, aiming for a bigger vision calls you to become the leader who will overcome more demanding barriers, inspires others to engage in change and fuels you through setbacks.

The shift: craft a vision that pulls you through obstacles

> 'We're here to put a dent in the universe.
> Otherwise, why even be here?'
> *Steve Jobs*

To succeed in leading transformation and making a dent, Mariví needed to make the vision bigger than the barriers, so that it would pull her through them.

It's your responsibility as a leader to craft a vision strategically in a way that:

- it's anchored in market, industry and company needs and opportunities, so that you drive a meaningful contribution that makes a difference and inspires others to buy-in.
- it's anchored in your strengths, abilities and successes, so that you connect with your capacity to deliver on it and rule out questioning about your legitimacy and credibility.
- factors in your values and aspirations to fuel you to overcome obstacles.
- factors in stakeholders' drivers and aspirations, so that you increase your chances to mobilize and engage others in change and navigate your way through people and organizational resistances to change.

Mariví needed to rise above obstacles and we worked on shifting her focus to the future she envisioned: the transformation she aimed to lead, how it would impact clients and her company, and how she needed to harness her talents and expertise to lead it. This enabled her to move beyond individual agendas and craft a competitive and inspiring winning case for her peers across divisions to bet on.

The key to success was communicating a shared vision in which each peer and critical player in her space could see the value of it to engage and buy into. For this, she needed to interact individually with each member in the room to uncover their drivers and common objectives and share her views of challenges and opportunities in the market to drive her division forward.

Setting a competitive vision by considering other players' drivers was the key to shaping a wider and more inspiring space in which her division could grow into. After applying these strategies for six months, she was put forward for promotion to Vice President and was promoted three months later.

Once you craft a vision for transformation and are ready to lead it, you need to keep an eye on how the next trait can trap you, hindering your progression and perpetuating the status quo.

Trait 3: Raise the bar and standards of excellence

You strive for mastery and the highest standards of excellence in everything you do.

Yet, the closer you get to what you want, the further away you feel and the harder you are on yourself.

To...
The High-performers
The Perfectionists
Those Demanding of Themselves and Others

To Pete

Pete was the Head of Operations for Europe, Middle East and Africa (EMEA) in at a multinational tech and social media firm. He surprised me on the first day with his commitment to his growth. He was hungry to know and experience what his peak looked like and was committed to figuring out how to improve, combining a humility and ambition that I admired.

He extended the same approach he had for his own development to his team and peers, raising the aspirations and standards of excellence in the units he operated.

He had made strides in his career operating this way, role after role, company after company, achieving higher roles of responsibility and impact; being recognized for his contribution and results by his team, peers and top management.

But when hitting a setback or not progressing as he would have hoped for, his growth system seemed to tremble and his confidence was hit. He started to compare himself to others and where he should be, and he questioned what he was after and whether he could achieve it.

He thought that to solve this and keep reaching higher, he needed to give more of himself. But the truth was that he needed to reassess how he was approaching growth.

A double-edged sword: achieving higher results can disconnect you from what's meaningful

"I did not get the promotion," Pete shared at the beginning of our session. "I would like to see how to bounce back from this setback and explore how to face what's ahead."

"And what's ahead?" I asked.

"I don't know."

When you're used to winning, excelling and going through hoops of growth as Pete did, it's not always obvious when you break that trend or you hit a threshold.

I recognized the frustration he experienced; that frustration that arises when there is a gap between where you're at and where you think you should be. Sometimes, regardless of what you achieve, your successes are weighted down by the expectations you have of yourself and others of what you should have accomplished, making that gap even bigger.

"I guess I'll just keep going," Pete shared, "although it feels like climbing Mount Everest every day."

"I understand you feel behind compared to where you wanted to be, Pete, but maybe Mount Everest is not the mountain to be climbing."

There is a misconception Pete had about success that I had observed in many other high-performers I had worked with – leaders who keep reaching higher but are disconnected to the meaning of their journey.

In my research about insatiability, I came across a concept shared by Tony Robbins, an American coach, that explains the dark side of this trait.

Robbins defines success as a combination of two factors: the *science of achievement*, which is the ability to transform what you envision into tangible results, and the *art of fulfilment*, which depends on the personal significance of the results achieved.[2]

He views the process of producing results as a science because it involves following a strategy, path or sequential steps to achieve one's vision, irrespective of its complexity. He considers fulfilment an art because what fulfils us is different and unique for each individual; in the same way that art is subjective, individuals attribute their own meaning and significance to their accomplishments.

If we map out these two factors, we have a grid of success at the intersection of achievement and significance with four quadrants that I drew with Pete in our session.

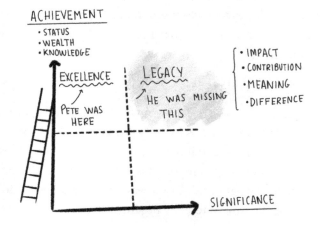

*In the vertical axis in the four-quadrant image, we map the
level of achievement*

As we climb up this ladder of success, we cultivate the
ingredients to produce higher results, and we grow in wealth,
respect, recognition, status, promotions, mastery, skilfulness
and knowledge, amongst other perks.

Leaders like Pete, who seek to grow in this vertical way, have
the capacity and abilities to create higher results for themselves
and their environment and are equipped and eager to operate
in more demanding levels of complexity and challenge.

But that's only a part of success for individuals and organizations.

*In the horizontal axis in the four-quadrant image, we map out
the level of significance*

As we lean into the right of this matrix, we operate at higher
levels of impact and contribution.

Exploring the dimension of significance requires leaders to
identify the meaning they want to give to their leadership and
personal journeys, the impact they can drive and the difference
they want to make. It requires them to take ownership of their
growth and take a stand on what they want to lead and how
they want to do it.

Pete would not stop taking notes.

"Pete, your capacity and habit of achieving higher results can limit your
individual and company success by only growing in the vertical axis
of achievement. This is essential for you and your company to reach
higher levels, but focussing only on this dimension can disconnect
you from exploring what's ahead in a way that's meaningful to you
and what can be meaningful to your organization."

Exploring significance requires time, intention and space for self-reflection. However, leaders like Pete are so tempted and used to succeeding by raising the bar of achievement that they can prevent themselves from leaning into the dimension of significance, thereby capping the success they can experience and the transformation they can lead.

The trap: you drift into an unfulfilling quadrant and distorted metrics

Climbing up the ladder of achievement is tempting for many leaders because it represents a clear path to advancement and progression that we all relate to:

more status + more wealth + more recognition, etc. = good stuff

We get attached to the perks of progressing on that path as we climb up the ladder. Not only do we get attached, but many people operate under those principles, standards and metrics, so they become our reference for progression.

The higher we climb, the more we become reluctant to move out of what's recognized, predictable or familiar into something that gives us more significance and meaning. This means that you risk settling for roles and projects that are respectable and recognized, reinforcing your reputation, sense of worth and status on a conventional path that does not inspire you and does not always ignite meaningful transformation in your organization.

Climbing up the ladder of achievement and excellence does not only limit company transformation and personal fulfilment. Measuring achievements according to conventional or recognized standards can trick leaders in how they assess their journeys, themselves and others.

As leaders climb up the ladder, they are reinforcing a metric system against which they measure their worth and progress that is distorted because it lacks a crucial dimension: significance. Not factoring it misguides them in evaluating their achievements, their worth and others' results.

Exploring this concept helped Pete understand that feeling of doubt and imposter syndrome that he and many leaders experience.

"Pete, when you don't experience success internally and don't connect to the joy of success despite all your efforts, it's because you're not connecting to what joy and success mean to you. This happens because you've not explored and are not operating in the dimension of significance."

"I realize I get my sense of competence and value from hitting targets and advancing projects across divisions and the recognition that I get," Pete said. "I've been getting through the hoops of growth like this for years, but there is always something else missing."

Leaders can feel they're an imposter in the world when in truth, they're an imposter to themselves because they fail to take ownership of their growth, their stand as leaders and the process of reviewing and re-defining their growth metrics.

"When you explore significance, Pete, your measures of success and progress change, the way you evaluate yourself and others change, your relationship with failure and setback change, and your demands with yourself and others change. You lead yourself and others differently when you're clear on the framework of growth you're operating. This happens when you've defined what's significant to you and what's relevant for the cause you're leading."

Leaders like Pete, with indescribable potential to make a difference, can be trapped in the game of excellence and climbing up the ladder, measuring their progress against metrics that make them doubt their worth. They exhaust themselves as they keep striving on a predictable path that is not giving them what they truly seek and what would drive meaningful transformation in their organizations.

After a number of years, leadership is a choice about what you're leading and how you're leading that. So, there is a moment where it goes beyond building competencies, growing in status and ensuring you hit targets, and it's about focussing on building a case anchored on what you want to lead and the difference you want to make.

Operating in the space requires leaders to explore the domain of significance. I'm all about achieving exceptional results and demanding high standards of yourself and others, but there is a quadrant in which you can hold yourself to such excellence and achieve results that are meaningful to you and your organization.

The shift: lean into significance and take ownership of your growth and metrics of success

"Once in a rare while, somebody comes
along who does not just raise the bar, they
create an entirely new standard of measurement."

Dick Costolo

To achieve ownership, you need to lean into the dimension of significance and define new metrics to lead in a new space.

This is about exploring:

- the legacy you want to leave in your organizations.
- the initiatives you want to put forward.
- the type of teams and cultures you want to nurture.
- the clients you want to serve.
- the relationships you want to build.
- the organization and industry problems you want to solve.
- what you want to experience in your career and life.

As you unpack these elements, you define new metrics to assess the progress and success for your strategy, yourself and others in this new space.

With Pete, we worked together to craft an entirely new role inside his organization. We unpacked what was missing in his career, his longings and aspirations and strategically explored his past professional experiences to find patterns to surface this.

He craved moving into strategy and defining a new roadmap and space in which the divisions he worked with and their team members could make bigger and more sustainable contributions. He explored the problems, inefficiencies and opportunities in these units and identified transversal changes required to catalyse next-level results with a customer-centric lens. He presented this vision to his Vice President and five months later, he stepped up as Head of Strategic Initiatives, creating a new global team from scratch and stepping into a new space of governance to drive change at scale.

Taking ownership of your growth can be challenging on its own. However, this challenge can compound when you immerse yourself in multiple growth challenges.

Trait 4: Multitalented, ultra-capable and overscheduled

 You're known for being at 130% of your capacity, immersing yourself with excitement and competence in new challenges, putting your talents to good use and developing new ones.

But you risk investing energy and focus on commitments that are not making a difference towards what you really want to achieve, limiting your impact, draining your energy and penalizing your well-being.

To...
Those On the Go
Those Who Are Versatile
Those Juggling Many Balls

To Lucie

Lucie had the energy and power of an atomic bomb condensed in her 1.6 m (5ft 3 inch) frame. She was about to start a role as an Executive Director in the Private Wealth Management division of a leading global investment bank.

She hooked me with her vitality and eagerness to grow, aiming to be on top of everything she had on her plate across many areas. Her schedule was packed with clients' meetings and industry events that she aimed to juggle with family and kids' responsibilities, spinning classes, and a pile of market trends reports she needed to read.

A few weeks into her new role, she was already involved in female leadership initiatives inside and outside her bank and collaborated with her EMEA Partner to upgrade the culture and talent initiatives in their division. On another side to all of this (if there was any room left in her schedule), she was looking to take Italian lessons and was looking for sponsors to bring French theatre plays to London.

She wished she had days of 30 hours to progress and excel with everything she had on her plate. However, behind a busy schedule and aiming to be everywhere and excel at everything, she was not driving the impact that her multifaceted essence wired her to. Her energy was suffering, her well-being as well, and with it, her leadership and performance.

A double-edged sword: busyness is not performance, nor impact, nor momentum

"I don't have time for everything that's on my plate," Lucie sighed.

I could see that one coming. As she walked me through her week and her calendar, I recognized that eagerness to be everywhere, do everything and engage in new challenges even before fully completing other open fronts.

Lucie's diverse interests and ultra capacity led her to get involved with excitement in new and diverse commitments across multiple competencies, achieving results quickly, and adapting and performing at new levels of complexity.

Versatile leaders like her are a source of fresh perspectives, energy and possibilities in their systems. They see connections and intersections between different fields to shape more multi-layered ideas and solutions, and they bring a breadth of knowledge to the multidimensional problems companies face.

But it has a dark side.

"Lucie," I said, "the risk of being multitalented is that you can end up doing everything, being pulled in different directions and being required by everyone as more opportunities can be a chance to learn, serve others or exploit your talents. And if they don't come up, you create them. The problem with operating this way is that these many commitments not only take up your minutes, but also your capacity to perform at the levels of efficiency, quality and impact you would like to."

Leaders like Lucie can spread themselves too thin and compromise time, focus and energy, resulting in capped levels of performance, efficiency, leadership impact and momentum.

These inefficient results occur because of two reasons:

i.   First, the 'quality' of their growth diminishes, impacting their energy to perform and their leadership capacity.

The value of a leader is in the choices they make and their judgement. Multitalented leaders like Lucie are equipped for this with the breadth of knowledge they bring, but as they stretch themselves, they deplete their energy and attention reserves. And as a result, they compromise the quality of their focus, leadership insights, well-being and performance.

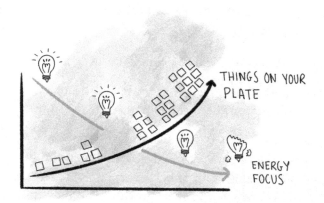

ii. Second, while they're in motion, their actions might lack
     transformative impact and momentum.

     As they engage in multiple activities, they distribute their
     units of energy across them, failing to fully invest them to
     drive impact and gain momentum to bring themselves and
     their company to new places in a significant way.

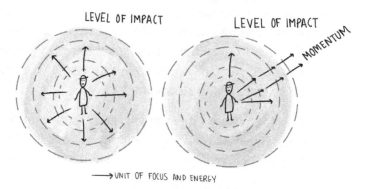

To improve her efficiency and performance, drive greater impact
and gain momentum, Lucie had to evaluate her commitments and
engagements, making the necessary adjustments to her calendar.
Nevertheless, this was counterintuitive to her nature of saying 'yes'
and packing her schedule, a pattern exacerbated by the ever-evolving
world of opportunities.

The trap: you add but don't adjust and are at the mercy of the environment

"If I take something out, I will be behind," Lucie confessed.

"But if you don't choose what's most relevant and adjust to the circumstances, you won't be ahead," I replied.

Leaders like Lucie, who are so used to attaining by saying 'yes' to challenges and opportunities, find it counterintuitive to pull themselves out of a rhythm they have practised over the years and which has contributed to their growth. And they think that if they choose one thing over another, it will penalize their sense of progression.

This trap is aggravated for two reasons:

- Leaders think they can do everything because they're multitalented. As a result, as they add to their calendars, their default pattern is to stretch themselves instead of evaluating external prompts strategically to reorganize their schedules.
- As they take on more commitments, leaders enter engagements with people. This introduces an additional layer of complexity as they refrain from adjusting their commitments to prevent any negative impact on their relationships or the perception others have of them or their abilities.

This way of operating can lead them to engage in patterns of guilt, pleasing or proving as they add and keep commitments that don't align with what would give them an edge or is relevant for their growth.

They can end up being a victim of their calendars as it can be difficult for them to rearrange their tasks and engagements because they don't want to disappoint others or themselves. This exacerbates their exhaustion and sometimes frustration for not having time for what they want to focus on next, leaving their paths at the mercy of what others require of them or circumstances.

The inefficiency that leaders experience from the previous trait of not taking ownership of their growth and their stand is exponentially magnified by them being in multiple projects.

Leading in changing and chaotic times involves continuously adjusting and adapting your decisions based on external and individual circumstances, market conditions and what you and your team need to perform in the frame of the vision you're leading, the difference you want to make and the results you seek to achieve. Instead of matching the frenetic pace of the moment that can exhaust you and cap your transformation and performance, you need to make strategic and conscious choices to decide what to say 'yes' or 'no' to and adjust as circumstances change.

To make these choices, you need to have an inner compass that centres you and guides you. Through this inner compass, you look through yourself to your environment and assess it strategically to choose where to invest your focus and time to drive impact while protecting your energy.

As leaders are pulled by the noise of everything they could do and potential new commitments, they're taken away from cultivating this level of inner diligence to observe circumstances and make choices from a centred place.

To change this pattern, you need to shift from an external focus to an internal focus; from attaining externally to attuning internally.

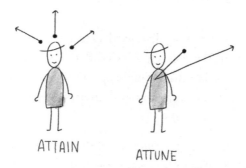

ATTAIN

ATTUNE

The shift: attune

Attuning means to make more aware or responsive and bring to harmony, as in the case of an instrument. It enables you to identify and assess discrepancies in your external and internal systems and adjust them to steer yourself and others towards better results.

Attuning consists of two stages: anchoring and choosing.

- **Anchoring**: you first need to deepen your level of awareness, on how you make choices and from which place you make them. You need to anchor yourself in your centre. Your centre is your stand and your criteria – what's significant and critical for advancement in the context of the market, the business unit you lead, your team members and your own well-being.

- **Choosing**: from this anchor or centre, you gain a new understanding of everything else in your context, seeing it through a new lens and making sense of tensions and demands in the framework of the vision you're leading and critical priorities. You observe and assess what's relevant in your calendar and what's not and rebalance it to create harmony and alignment between you and your environment, as you would attune an instrument listening to what's off.

To gain an edge in your leadership, you need to cultivate diligence at an inner level by grounding into your centre and bringing awareness to your choices to adjust and reorganize a calendar that supports your leadership.

I'm not implying that you disregard external demands. But if you don't anchor yourself in what makes a difference to guide choices and upgrade your calendar, then you'll cap the impact and performance you can drive in your company and environment and hinder your performance and well-being.

The choices are not always obvious, but they're much harder if you're not tuned into a level of inner awareness and anchored to the case you want to drive forward that helps you navigate a chaotic environment and make choices that support your and your company's growth.

> If Lucie was normally triggered by new stimuli to grow, this was exacerbated by starting a new role in a new company where everything and everyone was new and shone. Two weeks into her new role, Lucie was drained from navigating a demanding culture. We worked on consciously identifying the interactions, projects and habits that would advance her to take powerful steps in her first 90 days to position her as a reference in her division without jeopardizing her personal life and energy.
>
> As she tuned in to herself, she identified an untapped industry segment and worked on building a business case that would position her company as a reference in the market with solutions and strategies to engage top profiles of net-worth clients. This vision became her compass and anchor to strategically choose the potential clients, events and meetings to commit to for strengthening her strategy.
>
> Not only did she stand out in the EMEA space, but her vision and plan also crossed borders, and she presented her business case to the US management team.

Despite knowing that you need to take tasks off your plate, it's not always easy to step back. Your determination and reliance in your capacity to deal with everything can get in the way of this.

Trait 5: Self-reliant and determined

'Impossible' is banned from your vocabulary; you find the answers you need and you overcome challenges with little or no help from others.

But the higher you go, the more you're disconnected from the people around you, and fewer people are able to give you the inspiration, challenge and support you and your system need to transform.

To...
The Independent
The Resilient
The Gritty

To Elsa

Elsa developed her career in the advertising industry and was the Chief Executive Officer and Founder of an agency for Digital Strategy. She instilled a tenacity and conviction that she had nurtured from pushing herself to find solutions and surpass her limits in the toughest of circumstances.

She had nurtured her independent thinking and inner sense of confidence as she saw how her way of operating, decision-making criteria and standards advanced her system and opened new growth opportunities for her and others she worked with.

However, some people in her environment had different styles, views, standards and paces than her, and her manoeuvres for leading and engaging them did not result in the alignment, speed and buy-in she envisioned and needed to scale.

She would tap her self-reliance to keep pushing and progressing through obstacles because she needed to hit results, but consciously or subconsciously, she was depriving herself of the support, engagement, challenge and belonging she needed to make strides in her progression. She was stepping out of the conversations that held the clues and perspectives to propelling her growth and driving the progression she envisioned for her organization.

A double-edged sword: you lean back from the environment you need to grow

In her book *Grit*, American psychologist Angela Duckworth explores this superpower as the guarantor of success. She describes it as a special blend of resilience, single-mindedness, stamina, passion, effort and perseverance to stick to goals and your future, day in and day out.

Leaders like Elsa rely on their capabilities and their visions, their potential and their aspirations. They're a source of strength, effort and resilience to drive progress over barriers and inspire others to do the same.

But as leaders rely on their determination and convictions, they risk leaning away from their environment into themselves. This leads to isolation, limits their perspectives and increases the difficulty of connecting with other people who they need to engage with and gain trust from to grow at the levels they envision.

"Elsa, to scale and be competitive, you need others' ideas, views and energy to solve problems and shape more powerful and versatile solutions. Additionally, you need to engage others in change if you want to scale."

"I want to engage them," Elsa replied, "but they don't perform and rise to the level I need them to in order to deliver on what I envision. And sometimes it's easier to do it on your own, even if it's a bit isolating."

That burden was familiar, putting everything on your shoulders, even if you are burnt out, inefficient, lost or need help. The risk is that, sometimes, your self-reliance can trap you, blinding you to the possibility that there are other ways different from your own to generate results and engage others more effectively and impactfully.

"Elsa, as you lean back from the environment and tap into your self-reliance, you hide your perspectives and a part of yourself – your aspirations, struggles and ideas. When this happens, you decrease people's potential to connect with you, resonate with you, trust you and engage in your vision. You're perpetuating the results you want to change because you're not creating the conditions and conversations for others to engage with you."

Elsa was fixated on a story about others in her team not following, which she was using to justify the results she was getting and the lack of engagement she perceived. She would tap into self-reliance to keep going, but this prevented her from considering more resourceful strategies to mobilize and influence others.

I observe this pattern of leaning into self-reliance away from their environment in many leaders. Especially when there is a mismatch between their environment's mindset, pace, values, aspirations, ideas, agendas and theirs.

I observe this mismatch taking place when leaders try to navigate the political landscape and there are conflicting agendas or people resist change; when they experience that the culture does not promote disruption or agility; when they don't feel supported by their peers, management or colleagues in their aspirations or views; and when there is a lack of relatedness between their environment and their aspirations, challenges, pressures or responsibilities they face.

When leaders seek to navigate these situations and don't get the buy-in or support they would like or envision, they can lose motivation to engage their environment and disengage or disconnect from it.

Leaning into self-reliance patterns can be a survival tactic, a choice, an automatic pilot, a last resort or an act of stubbornness. And while it can get you progressing, your over-reliance on your capacities or principles prevents you from considering new strategies to interact and lead in your environment.

For example, the lack of commitment, engagement and support Elsa desired wasn't solely due to external factors that depended on others.

She was unaware of her ineffective communication strategies, styles and behaviours that failed to connect with others and engage them.

She was responsible for changing this, but her determination and self-reliance were hindering her ability to realize it.

The trap: it's more difficult to question your blind spots

The paradox of being self-determined is that you progress through thresholds but don't always see the limitations you have created for yourself.

Leaders who over-rely on their views and convictions reinforce a pattern of thinking and overcoming some situations on their own that prevents them from considering other alternatives.

As their self-reliance pushes them to achieve increased performance levels, usually outstanding, they don't feel the urge to question their ways of operating, deducing that they are achieving results after all. Or, in some situations, they have normalized things being hard.

To see their limitations, they need to be challenged and stretched from a new perspective. However, as they lean back from the environment, they deprive themselves of the support, challenge and inspiration from others to keep growing more impactfully and effectively.

This is exacerbated as leaders reach higher levels of success and step into new dimensions of challenges, responsibilities, pressures, aspirations and worries. As we grow, it can become more difficult to relate to our environment, be challenged by others and share worries or limitations honestly. The peak is higher, and the gap with other people's worlds is bigger; you won't trust everyone or be inspired by just anyone, and not everyone will be ready to challenge and stretch you to the level you need to reach higher.

However, if no one challenges your blind spots and how you approach pivotal situations for your growth, you over-rely on your views, your experience and your way of doing things. Not only does this hinder your advancement, but it also perpetuates a culture or environment you wish were different; for example, one with higher standards, a greater appetite for change, and increased agility and motivation to drive transformation. By distancing yourself from this environment, you reduce your chance and opportunity to intervene in it, upgrade it and inspire others to do the same.

To mobilize and upgrade her environment, Elsa needed to suspend the certainty and conviction that she had on her ideas, way of doing things and thinking about situations, and her capabilities. Only then was she able to create a space to question her blind spots and strategically explore others from a distance to engage them more effectively.

As you suspend the reliance on your convictions and focus on how others think and operate, you're able to gain new insights into their drivers and blockages. With this information, you can elicit new possibilities and uncover potential strategies to influence their thinking and elevate conditions in your environment to support your vision and aspirations.

The shift: lean in to upgrade your environment

By approaching your interactions with others differently, you can unlock potential outputs that you're not currently considering because of your self-reliance, putting everything on your shoulders or being anchored in your way of doing things.

You need to build an environment with people, practices and conditions that support your growth in the framework of the transformation you aim to accomplish and enable you and others to thrive.

This is beyond building a support network. You need to:

- coach your team members or direct reports to foster their autonomy and critical thinking to thrive and take the lead in more demanding situations.
- create units of excellence – teams, peer groups and culture – with conditions that promote transformation, diverse thinking, new ideas and excellence.
- develop a strategy to engage stakeholders inside and outside the organization in your vision.
- engage in conversations with allies that challenge your developmental edges and stretch you to reach higher.

To scale her agency, Elsa needed to build and grow a proficient team aligned with company goals.

As she was challenged on her blind spots, she recognized shortcomings in her leadership approach that hindered team engagement. She gained awareness of instances where her communication failed to convey her vision effectively and identified gaps in her ability to inspire, motivate and understand the individuality of what each person required to grow and be engaged. Equally, she assessed her team members' limitations, growth potential and drivers to surface new strategies to stretch their development.

She polished her political strategies to engage liked-minded players in her vision to scale. Reluctant to share her ideas and let go of control, she moved out of isolation and brought in a new partner with complementary styles and an investor who invested in the agency after seeing the potential of the business idea and a high-performing, versatile team.

These changes led to her tripling her annual revenue and the company went from a presence in one country to 12 countries. Her self-reliance enabled her to make progress, but challenging it led her to make leaps in her growth.

You need space to take perspective on your developmental edges and strategically assess your environment, and this requires you to stop and step back from your day-to-day race.

Trait 6: Sense of urgency to step into the future

When you see a possibility, you want to take immediate action and wish those around you followed your pace.

Your mind is on the future, and you find it counterintuitive to slow down and make adjustments to your priorities, habits or environment to get closer to your ambitions.

To…
Those Alert
Those Ten Steps Ahead
Those Without Time to Read This Chapter

To Alex

I met Alex for our coaching sessions at 8:00am in the morning. His energy was quick. His dialogue was rich and sharp. He put me in a state of alertness unlike any other client did. A second of silence looked like he was wasting time and he gave the impression he could not lose any.

He was the Sales Director of an IT and Cloud Services company. He had always described the sales division as the organization's growth engine. And I had no doubt his energy, ambition and essence were the fuel for growth in his company.

He had progressed astronomically in his career, having founded two businesses in the technology sector and led them through exit, the first one at age 25.

We started working together when he wanted to elevate his leadership with his team members and build solid foundations to scale his growth to get closer to executive management level in a large corporate.

Ironically, the fuel that had gotten him so far up was holding him back from this. He now needed space to gain new perspectives to strategically lead within his organization and develop his team members. For this, he needed to do the most counterintuitive thing for his system: slow down.

A double-edged sword: by going fast you sacrifice traction at scale in the system

"This week is crucial. We cannot lose momentum," Alex shared, speaking about his teams' race to hit targets. "We need to close three critical contracts and line up the new clients for next year's targets. I have two new members starting in three weeks; ace profiles, by the way, that I need to onboard. And there is a sales kick-off event next month to boost the unit for the sales targets and strategy for next year."

Alex had the capacity to open the door to his next few months in the first two minutes of the session. In his world of sales, his mind was always one semester ahead, visualizing new growth opportunities and the manoeuvres he needed to make to get there.

Alex embraced that part of me that lives in the future, excited about possibilities and potential growth, eager to become the person who would accomplish more demanding aspirations – often wishing things and people moved faster and results happened quicker.

Nolan Bushnell noted: 'The future doesn't come fast enough, so we need to pull it closer.'

Leaders with a sense of urgency to step into the future are visionary thinkers that anticipate trends and have a bias for action regardless of the challenging circumstances.

Saying that they adapt to change is an understatement. Their constant is change and motion. And they are equipped to be ahead in a paradigm of constant transformation.

However, speed is not the only factor that would put leaders ahead. By going fast, they can sacrifice driving impact in the systems they operate and, ironically, lessen the capacity to inject velocity in mobilizing other players in such systems to gain momentum towards collective progress as well.

Impact takes place when your actions benefit and grow the system you operate in – team members, peers, management, clients, stakeholders, culture and strategy. And momentum happens when you engage and bring that system forward with you.

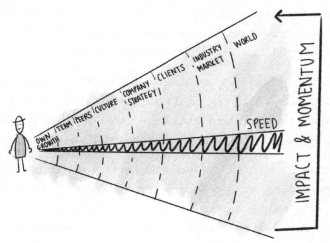

By going fast, Alex was just tiptoeing around the impact he could have in the system and the momentum he wanted to gain.

"You said you needed momentum this week, Alex," I said, bringing him to the present. "What would make you gain it?"

"Having my team empowered and switched on to close the deals."

"And why is that not happening as you would like?" I queried.

Alex gave this a thought for a few seconds (but not too many).

"To be honest… I'm playing for them, rather than coaching them to play better. I'm their voice of reason for critical choices and deals, so when they have a question, they come to me and it's easier and faster for me to answer those. However, they're not making these choices on their own, and their lack of autonomy ends up taking my time from other responsibilities…"

His focus was on making choices to move ahead quickly, and this was preventing him from investing time in developing his team members, fostering a high-performing culture and becoming a leader who would upgrade his system. He was sacrificing width over length, impact over speed, individual progression over system progression.

"To reach higher levels in the company, Alex," I said, "you need to operate at a wider degree in the system, investing time in growing and empowering your team, building partnerships, creating efficient units and participating in upgrading client solutions. If you're biased to making decisions and providing solutions quickly to keep moving forward, you're moving away from a deeper, more impactful intervention."

When leaders don't consider their system fully because they seek to catch up with the future, they won't drive impact in it. To impact and grow their systems, they need to assess them strategically to identify the interventions that would upgrade them.

However, to do this, leaders need to look at these variables in the system from a distance; they need to gain perspective. This cannot happen in the motion and speed of their day-to-day activities; that's why they need space. They need to step out of the scene they're operating in and consequently suspend the motion and progress.

But slowing down for F1 racers like Alex is counterintuitive, and this was exactly what prevented him from developing his team members and strategically making leaps in his impact to reach higher levels in the organization.

The trap: resistance to suspend your motion and progression

Some leaders wrongly believe if they slow down to create this vital space, they will penalize their growth. But it's precisely in that perceived suspension of progress where the secret for exponential growth lies, both for you and your wider system.

You need to be willing to suspend your false perception of growth and advancement to achieve something bigger for your system. This happens when you generate new insights to lead yourself, your business and others in new and more impactful ways.

For this, you need to hold yourself back from progression and reset your mind from a chaotic pace. This enables you to look at your system with clarity to maximize your insights.

To achieve this, I started every session with Alex with a breathing and body relaxation exercise. It probably felt like torture to him. I noticed how he resisted at the beginning like many other leaders who think that sitting still for three minutes won't make any difference to their growth. It does.

Applying the brakes to your bullet train and shifting down a gear drastically resets your state of mind and enables you to generate powerful insights in order to make leaps in your growth and impact.

The secret to exponential growth is creating the space to slow down and reflect from a strategic perspective with a clear mind. Alex needed to suspend his swim in the ocean to go into the fishbowl.

The shift: create space and go into the fishbowl

From within the fishbowl, you can strategically assess your system. You can visualize what's not working in your business strategy; you can see the inefficiencies in your company and identify the barriers stopping your team members from growing. You generate new insights and perspectives, and with those, you can dive back into the ocean ready to interact differently in your system to produce more impactful results.

The ocean has not changed, but you have.

To transform the system, you first need to transform yourself. To do this, you need to suspend your swim in the ocean to go into the fishbowl. Even if it does not seem you're progressing for some time, when you're back in the ocean, you will inject focus, intention and velocity in moving forward with your objectives and the transformation you want to lead.

Many leaders think that they can do this perfectly well swimming around within the ocean, progressing towards their destination. While it can make progress, the quality of the insights that you generate from stepping back enables you to make quantum leaps in your growth rather than increments.

The truth is…

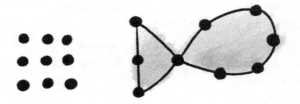

YOU CANNOT CONNECT THE DOTS...
IF THERE IS NOT SPACE BETWEEN THEM

Credit for the idea to Pejman Milani (@milanicreative)

The coaching sessions for Alex were exactly that: a space for self-reflection in which he would slow down to examine how he was leading his team. By the end of the programme, Alex had radically transformed the way he led his team members at a one-to-one level and as a group; he had become a coach.

With perspective, he could identify where his team members asked for his input in situations which they could handle independently. This enabled him to identify where they were tripping over their developmental edges to close sales deals on key accounts.

We explored the questions he could ask them to stretch their thinking to increase their ownership, autonomy and engagement. He changed the approach and structure of group meetings and led interactions with powerful questions to elevate the conversation and how the group was interacting. As his team members became more autonomous, engaged, aligned and stepped into their leadership, he was able to reorganize his team structure. He reduced his number of direct reports from 14 to 5. By focussing his one-to-one time with only these 5 people, he streamlined the team organization so that he could focus on new business opportunities while his organic growth targets increased 12% year on year.

Funnily enough, by slowing down, he created time after all.

Channel your traits

The six traits enable leaders to operate at their full potential when they exploit them, not only for their individual advancement but also to advance the system – business units, teams, peers, clients and culture.

Each trait needs to be channelled to optimize leaders in their development, maximize their contribution to the system and support new results.

In the next parts of this book, which cover the three-pillar elevation model and meta-abilities, you will find strategies to rise above the inefficacies of each trait to operate in a domain of increased growth and transformation continuously.

You'll gain new insights to channel each trait with the following intentions in mind:

1. Endlessly curious and unstoppable learners	Curate and own your intellectual property and ideas by fostering a curiosity with an inside-out lens to create a vision that drives impact in your business and positions you as an expert.
2. Think big and question the limits	Rise above barriers, naysayers, doubts and playing small games that promote the status quo to craft an inspiring vision for you and others that pulls you through obstacles.
3. Raise the bar and standards of excellence	Move beyond the domain of excellence, status and recognition to lean into the domain of transformation with new metrics for you and others to thrive in it.
4. Multitalented, ultra-capable and overscheduled	Instead of being at the mercy of the environment, upgrade your calendar and time choices to support the transformation you want to lead.
5. Self-reliant and determined	Challenge your developmental edges to see beyond your limitations and explore new strategies to connect with your environment and engage others in your vision.
6. Sense of urgency to step into the future	Create a space, develop a mindset and engage in habits that enable you to assess your system strategically and intervene in it.

Fundamentals

Here's your traits cheat sheet.

Bright side	Dark side	Trap	Shift
1. Endlessly curious and unstoppable learners			
Engine for innovation and advancement	Knowledge is not impact	Learning can be your comfort zone	Own your IP with an inside-out lens to curiosity
2. Think big and question the limits			
You question the status quo	You question yourself, the feasibility and your resources	You play a smaller game to avoid barriers	Craft a vision that pulls you through obstacles
3. Raise the bar and standards of excellence			
Achieve next-level results	Lack of significance and contribution	You operate in the domain of excellence with conventional metrics	Own your journey to take a stand on legacy and transformation
4. Multitalented, ultra-capable and overscheduled			
Fuel for advancement	Action is not impact nor momentum	You add but don't adjust and are at the mercy of the environment	Attune: anchor in your centre and choose
5. Self-reliant and determined			
You break through barriers	You recline from an environment you need to grow	You don't see your limitations	Upgrade your environment
6. Sense of urgency to step into the future			
You are ahead	Sacrifice impact and momentum in the system	Slowing down is counterintuitive	Suspend your ocean swim and go into the fishbowl (space to think)

Into the fishbowl: challenge your traits

 The questions below will enable you to explore and gain new insights about each trait in your developmental journey.

1. What's at the back of your mind that you've always wanted to lead, patent or share with the world (i.e. business ideas, an initiative inside your organization, a keynote presentation, a thought leadership piece)?

2. Who is getting similar results to what you want to achieve? Who are they being that you are not? What's the first step they would take that you've not yet taken?

3. What are you longing for in your life and career, and how do you keep it out (i.e. what choices are you making or not making to perpetuate this situation)?

4. What are the three projects, meetings or conversations that drain your energy or don't contribute to making leaps in progressing with your aspirations?

5. Who is getting the team results or the visibility that you would like to achieve? Who are they being that you are not?

6. What's behind the illusion that you don't need to slow down or create space to accelerate your growth and transformation?

Part II
Insatiable
elevation:
a three-pillar
model

Part II delves into the three-pillar model to help leaders channel the six insatiable traits to their advantage. It's designed to fuel transformation across the three dimensions of transformation – impact, performance and momentum – to create next-level results.

This model will help you to:

- **elevate your vision:** lever your ideas and talents to craft a vision that provides your business unit with a competitive edge and elevates your expert positioning.
- **elevate your identity:** stretch your abilities and mindset to operate at higher levels of complexity, excellence and challenge.
- **elevate your environment:** generate momentum in the system to overcome resistances and drive impactful change at scale by upgrading your interactions with your team members, peer groups and key stakeholders.

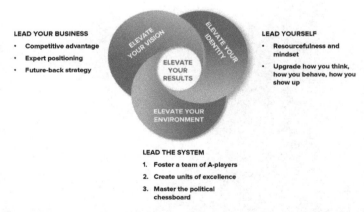

This three-pillar model is anchored in the following premise:

'Insatiable leaders develop in the process of producing extraordinary results framed by a vision that stretches and inspires them.'[1]

This means that the vision is the anchor that frames and fuels transformation across the other two pillars – identity and environment.

The coexistence of these three pillars elevates business, individual and system results.

This model is designed to serve any leader in any challenge or opportunity in their journeys. It invites them to frame and strategize their growth by referring to these guiding pillars to create next-level results.

As you think about this model to foster your leadership development, I invite you to picture that you're climbing a mountain, aiming to reach a peak, representing what you what to achieve next in your journey.

In any situation this model guides you to:

1. Raise your aspirations and stretch your vision beyond what you initially thought you could achieve – as if you were aiming for a higher peak. Operating under a stretched objective, enables you to set a more inspiring and impactful case of growth and transformation for your business, yourself and others.

2. Upgrade your leadership identity to become the leader who will lead that stretched vision at the highest standards – as if you were becoming a more competent climber to reach a higher peak.

3. Hone the conditions in your environment to generate momentum in driving your vision forward by upgrading your team and peer group to new growth thresholds – as if you upgraded the equipment to climb a more demanding or new mountain chain.

In the next few chapters, we will explore these three pillars with strategies to help you tackle them. Roberto, David and Sushant will be part of this journey as I weave in their stories and adapt dialogues to explain how they tackled each pillar.

Chapter 3

Elevate your vision

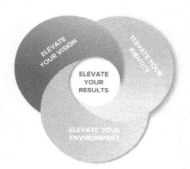

This chapter focusses on how to craft a vision that provides the business you lead with a competitive edge and elevates your expert positioning.

By the end of this chapter, you will uncover how to craft a vision that:

- maximizes your talents, ideas, perspectives and knowledge into a case that makes a difference in your industry, and you align with personally.

- positions your company as a difference-maker and elevates its competitiveness.

- positions you as a thought leader.

- maximizes your capacity to engage stakeholders.

- motivates you and fuels you through obstacles.

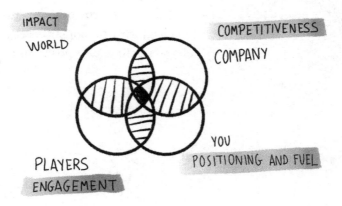

A vision that pulls you: transform yourself and your organization

'If you are working on something that you really care about, you don't have to be pushed. The vision pulls you.'

Steve Jobs

To Roberto

Roberto was a multidimensional leader. He had forged his essence by mastering the complex world of AI and quantitative methods, curating his resilience in the army, growing in comradery playing basketball and unlocking his creativity by playing music in a band. However, despite his brilliance, versality and multiple talents, he was not optimizing his potential.

Roberto was a Partner in AI and intelligent automation in a Big Four in Brazil, who had been transferred to New York. Despite being in the same company, he found himself facing a different set of rules in a more competitive political environment. In order to advance the AI division and be a critical player in this challenging new context, Roberto needed to establish himself as an expert both internally and externally, rallying team members, clients and stakeholders.

His mind was an AI library in constant update, on the edge of the latest trends. But his knowledge, ideas, talents and enthusiasm were neither translating into a powerful business case that would showcase his profile nor gaining buy-in from peers or support from management.

When I met him, he had recently been demoted from Partner to Managing Director due to a story around quotas and numbers, which added to his feelings of demotivation and frustration to raise his game.

Our engagement evolved around, basically, rising from his ashes! The spoiler alert is that after a year, Roberto was back being a Partner in his company, had hit his annual targets within the first six months of the year, had had four offers for Partner with competitors and had been a panellist in global AI summits.

Achieving this required him to relate differently to how he looked at obstacles, his positioning and his vision.

Push vs pull visions

The vision is the central pillar of every leader's journey, framing both individual and company growth. It provides a roadmap for success and objectives, has the potential to inspire and engage others in it, determines the type and level of results and promotes leadership development.

In accomplishing such vision, driving it and engaging others in it, there are obstacles and barriers in the journey that leaders need to overcome to bring it to life. They need to rise above misalignment, lack of resources, resistance from others to change, team underperformance, self-doubt or burnout, competing priorities and interests, lack of buy-in, clients' rejections, market recession, overloaded calendars – I'm sure you can keep going with the list.

You inevitably need to face those obstacles, but there are moments where they can take over your day and journey, making you feel limited or slowed down. When this happens, you can lose perspective on where you're going and narrow down your focus, reducing your sense of possibilities.

When leaders begin fixating on obstacles, they adopt a short-term future mentality, focussing solely on the immediate steps needed to progress in their journey. This can lead them to make their visions smaller and less ambitious, as they believe this approach will make it easier to overcome barriers.

What they don't realize is that shifting the focus away from the vision onto the obstacles is exactly what's blocking or slowing down their progress.

What will get them through these obstacles is having a vision that pulls them through. Having an inspiring and ambitious vision for them, their organization and others that enables them to engage clients, engage others and fuel them when they face setbacks.

The upcoming images illustrate the contrast between *push* and *pull* visions in overcoming obstacles.

When leaders focus more on the obstacles than their vision, they *push* the vision through obstacles in their journeys.

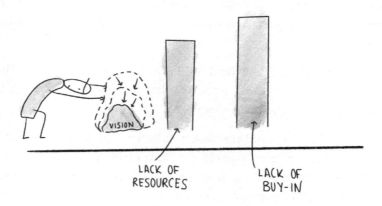

When leaders are connected to a vision that's inspiring and ambitious for their organizations, them and others, they're pulled by it. It acts like a driving force that is a counterbalance for obstacles, acting almost like a magnet that pulls leaders to the other side of them.

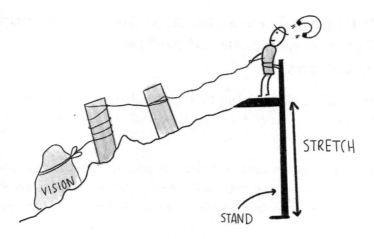

A pull vision is anchored in the stand or case you take as a leader, representing a stretch in the aspirations for you and others, and it's framed from the future to enable you to see beyond more demanding obstacles and consider alternatives to overcome them.

Roberto needed to create a pull vision that would engage others, elevate his competitiveness, represent an exciting case for his organization and peers, and motivate him to bounce back from setbacks.

A vision like this wouldn't land in his lap; he needed to craft it. This section explores the three strategies that will give you an edge in crafting and leading a pull vision:

i.   Define the **stand** you take as a leader that gives you an edge in your industry and elevates your expert positioning.
ii. **Stretch** your vision to inspire others and yourself to deliver on it and elevate your results.
iii. Shift your **focus** inwards to draw a pull vision and declare it from the future to implement it.

At the end of the chapter, you'll find an 'Into the fishbowl' activity to help you integrate the strategies.

Strategy 1: Take a stand: at the intersection of your organizational and personal aspirations

The stand you take is the business and leadership case you consider important to pursue at an organizational, industry and personal level.

To define it, leaders need to explore the difference they want to make in their industries and the problems they want to address and why. They also need to explore how they want to use their ideas, knowledge, perspectives and talents to make a contribution to their organizations and environment.

The stand provides leaders with a competitive edge by differentiating their views and criteria, elevating their value proposition, establishing them as a reference in their area of expertise and enhancing connections with those they want to engage.

It's the compass for their leadership decisions and strategies and becomes the core and centre of their relationship with their clients, their teams and peers, and themselves. It also frames their successes and failures, gives meaning and fuels their journey as they feel defeated. It's an 'all-inclusive'.

Despite its importance, many leaders have not explored it or are not connected to it in a way that would give them a competitive edge in their industries, their organizations or their own leadership strategy.

Without this stand, leaders keep progressing through their journeys, risking a drift from success to success, month to month and quarter to quarter, without taking full ownership of their journey or defining why they're in business. This limits their capacity to make a difference, gain an edge, fuel them through obstacles and engage others in their visions.

Not defining and connecting with his stand was limiting Roberto's capacity to elevate his positioning and raise his profile. He was not channelling the ideas, values, talents and knowledge into meaningful initiatives that would drive impact, position him as a critical player in his organization, engage others and advance his company.

To define his stand, he needed to look at his context strategically – including the industry, market and company – and explore his personal drivers and perspectives.

This section explores:

- the elements to craft your leadership stand – organizational and personal aspirations.
- how your stand can engage you and others to pull you through obstacles.

The elements to find your stand: organizational and personal aspirations

The stand you take is a case for growth and transformation you align to personally, provides a competitive advantage to your company and elevates your expert positioning.

You find it at the intersection of organizational aspirations and personal aspirations.

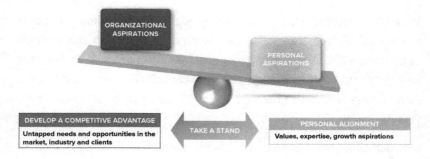

From one side, you need to explore what would represent an inspiring and competitive vision for your division or organization; one that would put it ahead of the competition and position it as a reference in your industry.

On the other side, you need to factor in your *persona* into what you're leading. This means that you need to factor in your values, expertise, ideas you care about and growth aspirations.

Let's delve into how to explore each of those elements and how doing so helped Roberto position himself as a reference.

Organizational aspirations: polish your expert lens to develop a competitive advantage

"I would like to become a reference within my organization and raise my profile outside it," Roberto stated.

"What do you need to do differently to what you're doing now to be seen as a reference?"

"I need to elevate the level of the conversations, making them more strategic. This will enable my peers and clients to start seeing my contributions on AI and automation topics not only as relevant but also as indispensable perspectives for their growth."

That's what being a critical player is, I thought.

To achieve this, Roberto needed to strategically explore the untapped potential of his industry through a new lens to gain the leadership edge he was looking for.

Strategically exploring your industry involves grasping and uncovering customers' expectations and unmet needs, along with identifying hidden problems or opportunities within your market. By doing so, you can develop innovative solutions to transform your sector, wow your customers and provide the business unit you lead or your organization with a competitive edge.

As part of this process, you also need to build a case towards company greatness by exploring what's missing or needs improvement in operations, people, procedures, digitalization, partnerships or culture to make your company more competitive as a 'unit' to gain an edge in the market.

The insights you seek in these areas have always been accessible; perhaps more so than you realize. You're standing on a mountain of gold that has the critical information to reach these answers. It's just a matter of shifting your perspective and looking at your clients, company and industry strategically and from a new lens.

This mountain of gold holds the key to finding your stand and shaping your case as an expert. It allows you to explore:

- the perspectives you've gained.
- the experiences you've had.
- the problems and opportunities you've observed in the market.
- the client conversations you've engaged in.
- the insight you've shared with your teams.
- the knowledge you've gained.
- the ideas and unfulfilled aspirations you've had on the back burner.
- the topics you care about and would like to address...

To define your stand, you need strategic questions to scratch the surface of your mountain, uncovering this information, and look at it from a new lens to gain new insights.

The questions below helped Roberto explore his **organizational aspirations**:

1. What's keeping your company ahead of the competition and a reference in the industry?
2. What's keeping your company away from being a first-choice brand in terms of solutions, processes and expertise?
3. What are the untapped problems or opportunities you see in your industry that, if solved, would wow your customers?
4. What is missing in how your clients are leading their strategy/operations/execution/people that keeps them away from being ahead of the competition and a reference in their industry?

You have the answers to these questions; this information lies beneath the surface of your mountain of gold as a result of your day-to-day activities and experience. You just need to look at it through a new strategic lens.

As leaders start considering these questions, they begin to delve into the unexplored realm of opportunities available for serving their clients, making a greater impact within their industries and upgrading their solutions and strategies. They start realizing that there is a space waiting to be tapped into for increased value for their businesses, prompting them to build a winning case for their clients, divisions and organizations.

When you explore the industry and market through this strategic lens, you realize what you pay attention to, what you value, what you think is important and your approach and criteria to solve problems. As you engage in this process you start polishing your expert lens to assess a situation and factoring in your personal criteria and persona. You can further explore these elements by exploring your personal aspirations.

Personal aspirations: elevating your expert positioning

Exploring your personal aspirations involves strengthening your connection, sense of alignment and significance to your leadership case at a personal level by factoring in your values, talents, expertise and aspirations.

It involves unpacking and factoring into your case:

- why you believe your leadership case is important for your clients, industry or team.
- the difference that your expertise, experience, insights, ideas and talents make to your leadership case or vision.
- your growth aspirations and the contribution you want to make in the frame of your case.

Exploring these elements is about intentionally explaining why your work matters, why it's important to you and how you can contribute.

For example, you can consider these questions to explore your **personal aspirations**:

1. What happens if the problem that you seek to solve is not addressed – what's the impact for your clients, industry or organization a month from now, a quarter from now, a year from now?
2. Why do you believe it is important to solve that problem now? What difference would it make to your clients, industry and organization a month from now, a quarter from now, a year from now?
3. What are the barriers to growth that your clients may be unaware of? What do you know that they don't? How can you help them?
4. If you were to deliver a keynote to a group of people, what would the topic be and who would those people be?

Answering these questions enables you to build a case not only for your clients, peers or company, but also for yourself. You explore what you care about and why you believe your case is important by emphasizing the significance of your work and identifying how your contributions make a tangible difference for your clients, the industry and your company. This process will help you personally connect with your case while also mapping out a strategy to position yourself as an expert to lead it.

Equally, factoring in these elements enables you to connect with others from a standpoint grounded in a larger purpose and case. This bolsters the quality of your conversations with clients, stakeholders and players in your industry.

> As Roberto explored his organizational and personal aspirations, he built a case to integrate intelligent automation into the core business. This involved moving beyond using automation for peripheral tasks or isolated processes and taking a stand to embed it deeply within the core operations and strategy of the organization and his clients.
>
> From this stand, he engaged with peers in other units that could benefit from using this strategy with their clients. He also identified topics for delivering keynotes to clients, sharing strategies about the untapped potential and pitfalls of AI that they were not aware of.
>
> He started to carve his area of expertise in the pharmaceutical sector, leading him to identify industry summits to boost his profile. Eventually, he participated as a panellist in a global pharmaceutical summit to discuss the trends in AI.

Exploring his organizational and personal aspirations gave Roberto a leadership edge amongst clients and peers. However, many leaders fail to strategically explore these two elements to shape their business and leadership vision.

Neglecting those can hinder your competitiveness, lead you to disconnect from the potential you could drive in your business units and organization, and diminish the inner drive you could experience.

As a result, your journey becomes less impactful, less inspiring and a bit harder to break through obstacles. The good news is that your stand can be the guiding force that pulls you and others through them.

At the intersection: engage others and engage yourself to break through barriers

When leaders define their stand at the intersection of organizational and personal aspirations, it enables them to increase their capacity to break through obstacles and engage others and themselves in it.

Engage others: value-based ideas that advance the system

As you factor in organizational aspirations, you're connecting to the world, the industry, the company and everything in that system. This includes stakeholders, peers, clients, team members and partners.

When you explore what would put your company or division ahead of the competition, or what are the untapped problems or opportunities in your industry, you're building a winning case for your business unit and organization. This increases your chances to engage players within that business ecosystem in a case that has the potential to make them advance.

As I worked with Roberto on his positioning, he would share how he sometimes felt competing agendas inside his organization that blocked him from finding consensus, moving forward in the same direction and gaining traction in promoting new initiatives. Like many leaders, he was put off or discouraged by this, when in reality, he had not undertaken the work to explore strategically the market and clients' needs. This prevented him from building an inspiring vision and a case that would enable others to succeed and, consequently, motivate them to buy-in.

There will always be competing agendas or ideas inside companies. What gives you a leadership edge is your capacity to shape a vision that factors in the needs, values and drivers of others and to find the intersection with yours, so that others see the potential to engage with you and bet on a bigger case.

Later in the book, in the section 'Master the political chessboard', you will find strategies to engage others in your vision and unpack their drivers to move beyond individuals' agendas and promote value-driven ideas that drive impact and foster partnerships. However, the initial step to engage others in your system involves exploring your organizational aspirations as part of defining your stand.

You need to explore organizational aspirations to aim for a competitive business case and engage others, but you need to factor in personal aspirations to fuel you.

Engage yourself: fuel to get through obstacles

Observing leaders navigating obstacles, I've noticed that their determination and commitment to overcome challenges stems from their desire to achieve success in projects and assignments they care about and where they feel confident and skilled to drive them forward. That's why factoring in your persona is critical to crafting a vision that pulls you through challenges.

As you explore and connect with your beliefs and drivers, what you care about, how you can make a difference and how business objectives contribute to your personal journey, you are invested personally in a case you want to bring to the other side of obstacles. Furthermore, anchoring your case in your strengths, experience and successes diminishes the questioning about your legitimacy or competence to deliver on it that might arise as you face obstacles.

You won't generate those insights miraculously; you need to strategically explore your organizational and personal aspirations. Only then will you be able to craft a vision that pulls you through obstacles, is competitive for your organization and yourself, and engages others and yourself in it.

The next strategy, 'Stretch', will give you an extra edge to elevate your competitiveness and make this vision more inspiring for you and others.

Strategy 2: Stretch: pioneer visions, pioneer leaders

'The greatest danger for most of us is not that our aim is too high and we miss it, but that it is too low and we reach it.'

Michelangelo

Not being connected to his stand was not the only reason that prevented Roberto from gaining an edge in his competitiveness and positioning.

Roberto's primary focus was on hitting his sales and utilization targets. Like him, many leaders can be easily trapped in their daily activities, targets and deadlines, with their focus on the next objective they need to achieve, setting them on a predictable path of progress. This leaves little opportunity for creativity and strategy to craft an inspiring vision that drives significant growth and transformation for both the individual and the company and inspires others within the system to engage in it.

Defaulting into a predictable next step or aiming for an incremental improvement in personal and company objectives can drive advancement and gradual growth, but this does not leap the company into new spaces and does not require a differential stretch in leaders' capacity and mindset to achieve such objectives.

When this happens, they're trapped in a default journey that prevents them from considering new possibilities that could bring themselves and their organizations to new places of competitiveness. When this happens, they're trapped in a box.

To propel themselves and their company to new spaces, leaders need to stretch their horizon of possibilities, raise their aspirations and think beyond their current day-to-day activities and predictable path of success to consider visions for themselves and their organization outside that box. Only then will they gain a competitive edge.

I refer to such visions as *pioneer visions* – visions that explore a significant, new alternative to a predictable trend of advancement, representing a non-linear path to growth for both the individual and the organization.

This section explores:

- what a pioneer vision is and the implication for your company and your individual growth.
- how leading a pioneer vision requires you to become a pioneer leader.
- the two considerations to craft a pioneer vision.

Pioneer visions: non-linear visions that lead you and your company to new places

A pioneer vision is a non-linear vision from the path and pace of progression that a company or leader follows. It represents a bet for company growth and individual transformation.

To craft such visions, leaders need to explore spaces and alternatives that they have not fully considered before. They need to break out of the box that limits their horizon of possibilities and contemplate a vision that seems 'impossible' for them and their organizations.

I don't refer to impossible as something unattainable, but rather as something that is beyond what they perceive to be currently achievable or have envisioned inside the box that prevents them from thinking beyond the predictability of their journeys.

Aiming to shape a pioneer vision requires leaders to stretch their thinking and operate outside it to consider new possibilities.

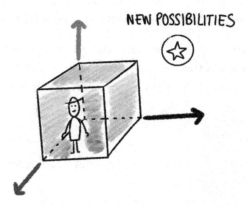

As you stretch your thinking into a new space of possibilities, you start exploring and considering a more ambitious and inspiring vision for you and your organization to grow into.

The key to achieving this is to move beyond the predictability of your day-to-day activities and the next logical step, and to intentionally draw out more ambitious aspirations. However, many leaders can be trapped in the pattern of predictable progression that prevents them from accessing this stretched thinking. Roberto was no exception to this.

In one of our first sessions of the year, I asked the following questions to Roberto to frame his development for the months ahead: "Roberto, where would you like to be by the end of this semester? What would you like to celebrate with me six months from now?"

"I would like to have hit sales targets and created new contacts to achieve that," he replied.

He knew me well enough to know that I was not going to let him get away with that answer. "Beyond targets, what would you like to achieve in the six months ahead for your growth and your division? Where would you have liked to lead your division, your team and your brand within the next six months? Tell me three critical players you want to connect with inside and outside your organization and why? Where are the spaces in which you want to be considered as an expert? And what would you have done to double your team performance by the end of the semester?"

With these questions, he was required to break out of his linearity and predictability.

As Roberto focussed on hitting objectives in the month ahead, he was setting himself up for lower results than he could create and was progressing on a predictable growth path. While this approach could ensure success and advancement, it detracted him from crafting an inspiring vision for both his personal and company growth. Considering these questions stretched his case beyond the respectable success he was achieving into a more exciting case for him and others.

He envisioned streamlining his team organization by reorganizing team units and reporting lines. Additionally, he prepared two leadership pieces to present in a breakout session on the inefficient use of AI to connect with new potential clients and elevate his positioning within the organization by making his knowledge more accessible to peers in other divisions. Furthermore, he strategized on building strategic alliances with finance and change management divisions to broaden his scope to drive a bigger transformation.

Ironically, by stretching his mindset beyond merely progressing with his objectives, he surpassed them. He hit his sales targets within the first six months of the year by aligning internal divisions.

The reason why Roberto surpassed his objectives is not only because he had stretched his thinking to set a pioneer vision, but also because he stretched his abilities to become the leader who would reach it. He had become a pioneer leader.

Become a pioneer leader

Your pioneer vision is not only a case of transformation to bring your organization to new places but also a case of transformation for you to stretch yourself and grow as a leader.

This is because the more ambitious the vision, the more you will be called to transform. As you stretch your abilities, you increase your transformational capacity in the organization; you become a pioneer leader – a leader who pushes boundaries and is at the forefront of innovation and driving organizational growth.

Let's explain this concept with a running analogy.

Imagine you're considering entering a course. You are not called to transform the same way if you're asked to run a 5K course in comparison to running a 30K one. What's needed from you in terms of training, upgrading your exercises and improving your eating habits is more significant.

Striving for more ambitious aspirations results in a degree of individual transformation that you would not have experienced if you had only set yourself a less demanding objective, like completing a 5K race. This analogy helps to illustrate the idea that even if you don't achieve your most ambitious aspiration of running a 30K, you will have evolved into an athlete capable of finishing a 20K race and performing at that level of challenge.

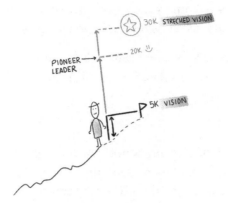

This running analogy applied to leadership and business transformation suggests that leaders develop and transform in the process of aiming for a pioneer vision that stretches them and inspires them. Through this journey, they evolve into pioneer leaders equipped to operate at a higher degree of challenge, advancing their organizations and fostering their competitiveness as individuals.

For leaders who are driven by growth, as is the case for insatiable leaders, operating in the framework of a stretched challenge is critical for their engagement and motivation. Incremental objectives don't represent an inspiring challenge for their growth, diminishing their motivation to grow and fuel themselves through obstacles. Defaulting into the next logical step or aiming for what's reachable can be like kryptonite for these leaders.

The key to motivating, retaining and engaging leaders with a bias for growth is to develop them in the frame of pioneer visions that inspire them in their growth journeys.

Considerations to craft a pioneer vision

To craft a pioneer vision, you need to raise your aspirations. This requires you to explore a dimension of (im)possibilities where you can create more powerful, impactful and fulfilling results for yourself, your company and system.

To succeed in stretching your vision, and setting and sustaining it in motion, there are two considerations you need to have in mind:

i.   Your pioneer vision needs to be genuine.

ii.   Pioneer visions means more obstacles and fewer references.

Genuine visions

The importance of a vision is not that it is big but that it's genuine, anchored to what matters to you. This means that a pioneer vision needs to be anchored to your leadership stand.

When you stretch your aspirations on the stand you take, you maximize and reinforce the power that your stand has in crafting your vision. From one side, you increase your capacity for making a bigger difference and, on the other side, you stretch yourself into a space of possibilities of something you care about, reinforcing the power that your vision has to pull you through obstacles.

However, if you miss the first step of defining a stand, the stretch can be counterproductive. Stretching on a vision you're not connected to will magnify the sense of disconnection, leading to frustration, demotivation and even pressure. This is because pursuing a bigger vision will inevitably lead to encountering more demanding obstacles, but if you don't align personally to it, you won't have the fuel of a stand that pulls you through barriers.

Before stretching your vision, you need to define your stand.

Pioneer visions means more obstacles and fewer references

As you pursue pioneer visions that are non-linear to your predictable growth path, you'll not only face more demanding obstacles, but you may also have fewer references on the steps to take.

Pioneers are the ones to explore a new domain or space, and consequently, there will be fewer references for you to consider or metrics to measure yourself against.

As you stretch yourself out of a non-linear path, you must redefine the metrics of success and progress, and reorganize yourself and your environment in a new space.

Still, many leaders can hold off on taking decisive actions on their visions because they want to know if they're on the right track. They may compare or measure themselves to others' standards of progression that are not pertinent to the stand they take and the vision they seek to implement, which blocks them in their advancement.

That's why, as a part of setting a pioneer vision, you need to develop a strategy to map the key milestones to progress with your stretched aspirations solidly and strategically. The key to crafting a pioneer vision and implementing a powerful strategy to lead it lies in where your focus is.

Strategy 3: Focus: an inward journey, a future declaration

'It always seems impossible until it's done.'

Nelson Mandela

The expectations from this chapter are high in terms of creating and leading a vision that has the power to pull you through obstacles. You need to aim for a stretched vision that drives you and your company forward on a non-linear growth path, increases your impact, fuels you and engages others.

How do you craft that vision? And then, how do you lead it in the real world?

The clue is where the focus is. You draw from within, shifting the focus inwards and exploring strategically how you connect with critical information about the market, yourself and others. And you lead it from the future, shifting your focus to a place where you have overcome obstacles and achieved success, allowing you to gain new perspectives to develop your strategy.

These are the shifts that enabled Roberto to gain the insights to elevate his competitiveness and rise above obstacles. Let's explore each of those lenses in detail.

Drawing your vision: an inward journey

A pioneer vision is non-linear to your individual and company growth path. This means that you won't achieve it by considering the next logical or predictable step; instead, you need to craft it. The good news is that the inspiration and clues are inside yourself, so you need to draw it from within by turning the focus inwards and engaging in introspection.

Remember that you're standing on a mountain of gold, with information about the market, industry, customers, your values and your knowledge that's waiting to be harnessed and optimized into elevated leadership insights and impactful initiatives. Successfully engaging in strategic introspection involves:

- Surfacing and unpacking the information of your mountain of gold.
- Gaining new insights about how the information connects and its potential for transformation.
- Reframing those insights to shape a pioneer vision.

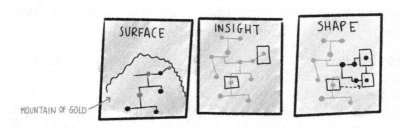

The questions at the end of the chapter are designed to help you in this process. Once you start collecting the information, the next step is to bring your focus to the future to declare your vision, stretch it and develop a future-back strategy that sets you in motion.

Declaring your vision: speak from the future

Bringing your focus to the future involves speaking from a place where you have achieved the pioneer vision you're aiming for.

This is not about visualizing from the present to the future. Through this lens, you might end up seeing obstacles ahead or might be tempted to aim for the next logical possible step, thereby limiting your perspective about alternative ways to drive more impactful transformation.

Instead, shifting the focus to the future requires articulating, in present tense, what success looks like as if you had already accomplished it. From this place you can work backwards from your vision, also speaking about obstacles as challenges you've overcome.

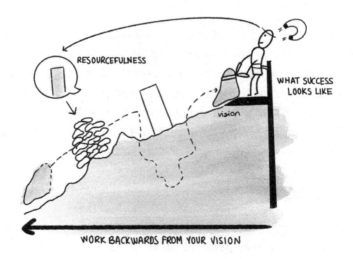

This shift is critical to lead pioneer visions and become a pioneer leader for two reasons:

i.   When you position yourself in a place where you've achieved success in the future, you step into a space of new 'impossibilities' that you had not fully explored before.

ii.   You tap into your resourcefulness as you look at obstacles from a new lens.

New 'impossibilities'

As you fast forward to the future and connect to what success looks like, you reveal new possibilities to set a more ambitious vision for you and your company, simultaneously connecting to the impact that achieving this vision has on your business, yourself and others in your system.

The power of this strategy is that by articulating new results and 'impossibilities' outside your box from a future perspective, you make a pioneer vision more tangible and clear in a way that you could not elicit from the present. This is because you've moved beyond obstacles or a short-term mentality that prevents you from thinking strategically and ambitiously.

For example, when I asked Roberto to explore where he wanted to have led himself, his business unit and his team *six months from now*, he was required to clarify what that future looked like. Likewise, you can set ambitious visions for you, your company and your system, clarifying what you want to have accomplished three months from now or a year from now. As you think this way, you move beyond the predictability of your journey to explore stretched possibilities.

Resourcefulness

When you speak from the future, from a place where you have achieved success, you perceive obstacles differently. Rather than viewing them as barriers you still need to face, which is what you perceive when you speak from the present, you look at them through a lens as if you had overcome them. From this standpoint, you're required to work backwards from success and your vision to elicit the strategies and critical steps that have made overcoming these obstacles possible.

A shift in perspective enables you to look at any problem differently. Speaking about obstacles from a perspective where you've gone through them enables you to gain new insights about ways to tackle them, thereby fostering your resourcefulness as you reveal new possibilities to take action.

From the future, you can create a non-linear future-back strategy that enables you to identify how you need to lead yourself and others differently to succeed in achieving your vision.

Fundamentals

- There are visions that you **push** through obstacles and visions that **pull** you through them. To craft a vision that pulls you, you need to:

    i.   Take a stand

    ii. Stretch it

    iii. Adjust your focus to draw it and declare it

- Your **stand** is a case for transformation you align with personally. It provides a competitive advantage to your company, elevates your expert positioning, engages others and fuels you. You find it at the *intersection of organizational and personal aspirations.*

- **Stretching** your vision requires you to aim for an ambitious and inspiring case that transforms you and your organization. As you step beyond the box that limits you, you lead a *pioneer vision and become a pioneer leader.*

- You shape your pioneer vision by drawing it from within, turning your **focus inward** and exploiting the information in your mountain of gold.

- You lead it and declare it by speaking from the **future**; from a place where you have achieved success and overcome obstacles. This enables you to explore more ambitious possibilities and tap into your resourcefulness.

Into the fishbowl: draw and declare a pioneer vision that transforms you and your company

 The following questions will guide you to integrate the insights from this chapter and elevate your positioning and competitive edge. The steps are inspired by the tactics to construct a perfect pitch in the book *Key Person of Influence* by Daniel Priestley.[1]

1. **Articulate your case:** what problems or opportunities do you observe in the market to advance/transform your industry and/or wow customers? Which one of them, if addressed, would triple your individual and company's competitive edge?

2. **Extrapolate on the impact of not solving the problem:** what happens if the problem or opportunity is not addressed a month from now or a year from now? What will the impact be on your company, customers and/or industry if it's not addressed?

3. **Solve it**: what is the solution you suggest? What's the roadmap to success?

4. **Establish credibility**: what experience, connections, results and expertise back you up and make you/your team/your company perfect or equipped to deliver that solution?

5. **Leave people uplifted and connected to possibilities**: a year from now, what has been the difference you have made in your industry or with clients, and how did you achieve it? What has been the *before* and *after* in implementing your solution? *Use the present tense as you respond to these questions.*

If you prefer, you can complete the sentences below:

- *The impact this solution is having on clients' businesses/in the industry after one year is...*

- *What they have achieved thanks to this solution that they could not have achieved a year ago is...*

- *The problems they did not know they had, but we are now addressing are...*

- *The three key obstacles we overcame this year to achieve this were...*

Chapter 4

Elevate your identity

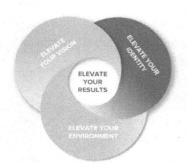

Within this chapter, we'll explore how to become the leader who will bring your pioneer vision forward.

Leading a stretched pioneer vision requires you to become a new leader.

When you introduce an element of non-linearity in your vision beyond pursuing the next predictable objective, you need do something substantially different to deliver on that vision. This means that you need to develop new ways of thinking, behaving and showing up in your day-to-day situations to enhance your performance and create next-level results within a more challenging context.

The reasoning looks straightforward, but the application is not.

As we explored in the first part of the book, at any moment in time you're trapped in a box that can frustrate your efforts to create new results and lead in a new context, and the only way to reach significant new growth thresholds is to break out of it.

By the end of this chapter, you will:

- understand what's trapping you in a box and holding you back from elevated results in situations critical for your growth.
- learn how to stretch your mindset and upgrade your behaviours to break out of it, enabling you to overcome barriers and generate opportunities for increased resourcefulness as you increase demands and aspirations.

This chapter has been inspired by the work of Dough Silsbee, founder of Presence-Based Coaching®, on identity, habits and self-generation.

Why do we need to change? (even if we are successful and ultra-capable)

> 'Knowing yourself is true wisdom.
> Mastering yourself is true power.'
>
> *Lao Tzu*
>
> **To David**

I met David for the first time in a café by Monument station in the heart of the City of London.

We met at 8:00am before his day started. David came in through the door with his briefcase, looking polished, sharp and slightly rushed.

He intrigued me. I could breathe his essence of success, aspiration, eagerness and self-reliance with a touch of unsettlement and disturbance. His eye-contact was evasive at the beginning of our conversation. I noticed his discomfort, or maybe lack of practice in acknowledging that he had reached a glass ceiling he did not know how to break through.

He had been working for more than a decade in a Big Four. Due to his excellence, results and track record of success, he was about to be promoted to Partner in the insurance division in the UK.

Wholeheartedly he shared how he found the promotion to Partner a bit daunting, stepping into a completely new space with different game rules, metrics and requirements.

With similar questions I shared in the previous chapter, we worked together to elevate his vision and shape a competitive Partner case to strengthen the insurance practice in the UK and scale it to EMEA. However, this was not the only strategy he needed to succeed in this new space.

In a subsequent conversation, he shared how he wasn't getting where he wanted with a calendar hijacked by client meetings, team meetings and one-to-ones. He was dedicated to excelling at project delivery by managing client deadlines, budgets and team performance, but he was not focussing on shaping the strategy to elevate his positioning as a Partner nor leading his team to support his growth in a new space.

David was trapped in a box to create new results. He was relying on the strengths that made him stand out as a Director, but these would not give him an edge as a Partner. If he wanted to thrive in this new space, he needed to evolve into a new leader and harness differently these strengths, even if they had made him successful.

Lessons from winners: the limitations of your strengths to conquer a new space

In the book *Everything can be Trained* (*Todo se puede entrenar*) by Toni Nadal, Rafael Nadal's uncle and coach at the time, Toni shares a story about how Rafa needed to evolve into a new player.

Between 2005 and 2008, Nadal won four titles at Roland Garros in a row, the only Grand Slam titles he had won up to then, showcasing his talent on clay. However, Nadal did not only want to be the best on this court surface, he also craved to conquer the grass surface and win a title at Wimbledon.

While his success on clay was unquestionable and his competencies as a tennis player were undeniable, the truth was that the abilities that had crowned him on clay were not playing to his advantage on grass.

Toni explains how the grass was a different space: the court was different, the game was quicker and the competition played out differently, benefiting players more suited to excel on grass and revealing Nadal's limitations on this surface.

The grass also had its king – Roger Federer, who had won five Wimbledon titles in a row by 2008.

If Nadal used his abilities and winning strategies on the grass the same way he used them on clay, he would not conquer Wimbledon. Doing more of what he had been doing would not give him an edge on grass. He needed to adjust his techniques to adapt to the speed of the ball and counterbalance his limitations on grass. And he needed to be equipped with new technical and mental strategies if he wanted to win.

Nadal and Toni worked on Nadal's blind spots and limitations and upgraded his game to excel on grass. In June 2008, Nadal won his first Wimbledon title against Federer.

David came to mind when I read this story.

The Partner space revealed his limitations and inefficient ways of operating in his day-to-day situations with the strategies he was using, even if they had made him successful before. Without realizing, he was trapped in a box of habits and conditioning that he needed to break out of.

The reason for this was his leadership identity, and if he wanted to achieve significant and new results, he needed to understand how it functioned to upgrade it and support the results he envisioned.

The coming sections explore the steps David needed to follow to achieve this and that you need to tackle as you seek to elevate your results in new or more demanding situations. These are:

    i.   Meet your identity and the box that traps you in.
    ii.   Surface your identity.
    iii. Upgrade your identity.
    iv. Reinforce your new identity.

In the last section of this chapter, you'll learn how these steps need to iterate to create next-level results continuously.

At the end of the chapter, you will find questions that helped David tackle them, which you can consider for your growth.

Step 1: Meet your identity and the box it traps you in

The biggest obstacle preventing leaders from creating next-level and new results is that they have not gone to the core of how their inner system 'fabricates' results. And, more importantly, how their system prevents them from raising their game and elevating their behaviours in the face of a new challenge or vision.

As leaders aim to elevate their performance, they seek to explore new strategies and insights that would enable them to interact differently with their clients, management, peers and stakeholders, and lead their responsibilities more effectively. However, these strategies don't always enable them to make the leap required to create new results or sustain them, thus blocking their advancement, slowing them down and frustrating their aspirations.

The question they're usually after to overcome challenges and aim for new growth thresholds is: 'What do I need to do to achieve higher results?'

Nevertheless, the question that would give them an edge in their growth is: 'What's holding me back from elevating my results and sustaining them, despite my efforts to achieve this?'

To answer this, you need to understand that you're trapped in a box and why you're trapped inside it. This requires you to comprehend the intricacies of how you operate, which are influenced by your identity and habits. Once you realize how they function, you can intervene in them to upgrade your results.

Your box explained by your identity and habits

Let us explore these two concepts and how they're interlinked.

Your identity is your self-conception and collection of ideas, beliefs and perceptions. It's what you hold to be true about your experience and yourself at any given moment, based on your own developmental journey, background, context, history and experience.

It determines how you describe yourself as a person or the type of leader you consider yourself to be. It also shapes and determines, for example, your perceptions of reality, how you look at yourself and others and your horizon of possibilities, which represents what you consider to be possible or achievable at any given moment.

In this chapter, you will comprehend how these elements are behind how you respond to situations and the results you create. But first, let's delve into the concept of habits.

During your journey, parallel to your identity formation, you've developed habits – the responses and behaviours you have learnt to engage in.

You should know that these habits are deeply engrained in your system, not only at a behavioural level, but also intertwined with emotions, body conditioning and a story of interpretation of reality that determines your behaviours and the results you generate.[1]

These habits are part of who you are and dictate how you show up and behave in situations with your clients, team and peers, as well as how you respond in your day-to-day activities and to the challenges and opportunities that lie ahead.

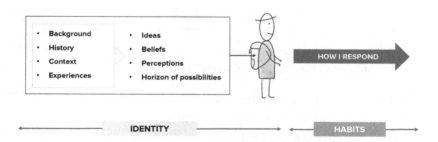

Your habits comprise your way of being in the world and they are at the service of your identity, not always at the objectives you want to achieve. That's when your problem to achieve new results starts.

In any given situation, you will be drawn by your identity and the habits you've learnt to engage rather than behave in ways that will lead you to the results you seek to produce. In other words, you're trapped in a box away from what you want to achieve.

To engage in different behaviours that lead to new and next-level results, you need to understand how your habits and identity function in any given situation to dismantle this system and break out of your box.

Your identity and habits in action

Understanding how your identity functions is the clue to rising above obstacles in situations in which you feel limited, frustrated, slowed down, blocked or inefficient, or where you're not maximizing your performance within your teams, peer group or client interactions.

The first step towards new results is identifying the situations in which you want to raise your game. This was the first step David needed to take.

> David wanted to show up differently in team meetings and conversations with stakeholders.
>
> On one hand, his political landscape had changed, and he wanted to navigate it strategically and demonstrate his competence as a Partner with new players. On the other hand, he wanted his team members to step up and take on more responsibilities so that he could focus on shaping and implementing his Partner strategy and raising his visibility amongst new stakeholders. However, they still relied heavily on him to deliver on client projects.
>
> Despite his intentions to raise his profile as a strategic player, he found himself continuously gravitating towards conversations and manoeuvres centred on client delivery and projects, moving him away from his strategic aspirations. He was trapped in a subconscious habit that he needed to address if he wanted to change this.

What would give you an edge in your leadership development is understanding how your identity operates in each situation so that you can intervene in its functioning and upgrade it. The image below illustrates this.

Doug Silsbee explains how your inner system responds in a situation and how it determines the results you get.[2]

- In a specific situation, there is an event or **trigger** that happens around you that evokes a response in your system. It can be anything: someone's reaction, or expression, a topic brought to the table, a request from another person, a question, the tone in the question. Anything.

- Your system responds internally to this trigger at three levels:
    i. **Somatically**: based on your body conditioning at a very subtle level, observable as tightness or energy, usually going unnoticed if you have not developed body awareness.
    ii. **Emotionally**: based on the personal significance that you attach to it, influenced by your personal story, experiences and background. This response is observable as an emotion that determines the quality of your state (disappointment, joy or contentment, for example).
    iii. **Mentally**: based on your interpretation of that trigger, emerging as stories, judgements or evaluations about the situation and the people involved in it.

- These internal responses are interrelated and their connection happens rapidly, cascading in a **behaviour**, which leads to a **result**.

This is how your identity influences the results you generate in a situation: you respond internally to a trigger – somatically, emotionally and mentally – which in turn results in a behaviour.

While assessing your inner responses might look more complex than just considering how you need to behave differently, it's critical that you understand what's behind these responses, as they're the ones responsible for keeping you trapped in a box. In other words, operating at the root of your inner responses is what will give you an edge in your leadership, and for this you need to understand the system of attachment and aversions under which your identity operates.

A system of attachments and aversions

Your identity that orchestrates those inner responses operates under a system of attachments and aversions.[3] Attachment to what you want or what you hold as positive, easy or familiar based on your experience. Aversion towards what you want to avoid or what you hold as negative, difficult or unfamiliar.

For example, attachment towards recognition, wanting to be seen as competent or legitimate. And aversion towards being seen as a failure, fear of rejection or putting boundaries on others. These drivers can operate at a very subconscious level and these are just a few examples that manifest differently for every individual depending on what they hold as 'positive' or 'negative' based on their identity.

What's important for your development is that this system of attachments and aversions is responsible for driving your internal responses and behaviours that lead to results. This means that you engage in specific internal responses and behaviours depending on what you subconsciously want to reinforce or is familiar, and what you subconsciously want to avoid or is unfamiliar.

Your results can be at the mercy of this subconscious mechanism if you're not aware of it. When those results are not aligned or are inefficient in the frame of your vision or objectives, you produce **unintended results** – which are the results David wanted to change in his meetings.

The implication of this for your growth is that if you don't gain awareness about what is subconsciously driving your responses and you don't intervene in it, you'll engage in almost the same responses in similar situations. As a result, you develop a habit that leads to similar, unintended results repeatedly, defaulting into a **habit loop**.

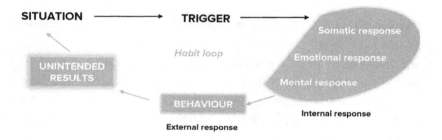

This habit loop is the one that keeps you trapped in a box.

Operating under the influence of this habit loop was leading David to always interact with his team members and stakeholders the same way, despite him wanting to show up differently. His habit loop was leading him towards similar results in his meetings when he wanted to raise his profile as a strategic player and engage in new conversations.

To dismantle this habit and break out of his box, he needed to surface his identity and intervene at the level of attachments and aversions.

Step 2: Surface your identity

Surfacing your identity involves understanding how you think, behave and respond emotionally to any situation and the subconscious drivers and habits behind your responses. Only then you'll realize what prevents you from achieving your desired results.

The key is to get to the core of what's at stake for your identity, sometimes at a subconscious level in each situation. However, succeeding at intervening at this deep level is not a straightforward process.

As you scratch into the core of who you are, you start unpacking what's holding your identity in place. You probe your value systems, views about the world and images you hold of yourself that you need to challenge and transcend to break through them. Equally, you surface longings and deeper fears, such as longing for approval, fear of losing status and fear of accepting your limitations or sharing them.

Intervening at this level of values, fears and longings is critical because it's what holds your identity in place and traps you in a box. But it is not always obvious. It involves engaging in an honest and vulnerable process of accepting your limitations and views about yourself you might not want to see or recognize. Equally, it also requires you to challenge your approach to growth and what has made you successful: your winning strategies.

Your winning strategies

Your winning strategies are the ways of operating that have proven to be successful in achieving your objectives and that you rely on to achieve success.

As promising as this sounds, they can block you to reach new growth thresholds and trap you in a box, if you don't channel them strategically. This can be counterintuitive, but they can become a double edge-sword for your progression in the same way that the traits that we explored earlier in the book do, and in the same way that Rafa Nadal's abilities on clay would not give him an advantage on grass.

As is the case with the traits, the winning strategies that you rely on for success can also be limiting. Each leader has their own and identifying yours as you surface your identity can give you an edge to understand why you're trapped in a box.

> As David reflected on how he led his conversations with his team and peers, he realized he was comfortable at operating at a tactical and operational level. He realized that as Director he had been

used to harvesting successes by excelling at managing project deliverables and looking at projects through a technical lens. As such, he guided teams in generating answers and solutions under a defined scope that enabled him to track progress.

He excelled in operating this way, reinforcing his identity of being a competent leader. In delivery, exploiting his tactical and operational 'winning strategies' led to observable progress from one week to the next, reinforcing his sense of confidence and competence. However, to thrive as a Partner, he was required to engage in more strategic projects, measuring progress over a timeframe of three to six months.

The Partner space felt daunting because he feared how he would be valued and recognized for leading strategic projects. To protect his identity as a competent leader, his inner system was 'triggered' when he saw an opportunity to prove his competency, defaulting into a 'habit loop' to engage in conversations about delivery and technicalities. This pattern moved him away from engaging in conversations about strategy that would give him an edge as a Partner.

William Edwards Deming, an expert in the fields of quality management and process improvement, quoted that: 'Every system is perfectly designed to get the result that it does.' And David's wiring was perfectly designed to get the unintended results he was getting:

- His identity craved the feeling of competence and influenced his ineffective behaviours and results.
- This subconscious need was so deeply engrained that it outweighed his conscious objectives and aspirations to grow and raise his game in the Partner space.
- His habits and responses were perfectly designed to validate his competency and he achieved this by doing what he did best: focussing on delivery, technicalities and tactics. Those were his winning strategies in action that were triggered

when his competence was at stake and that perpetuated him to continue in a habit loop.

While they enabled him to create results and reinforce his sense of competence, over-relying on them prevented him from exploring new behaviours and strategies to thrive in the Partner space and create new results.

Realizing that winning strategies are a limitation to growth was not an obvious step for David as is the case for many leaders.

Accomplished and successful leaders can be so attached to their winning strategies and their views about how they approach growth that they cannot see, or don't want to see, how these trap them in a box. And the only way out of it is by challenging them.

Step 3: Upgrade your identity

If a habit loop led David to unintended results, then to upgrade his identity, he needed to find an alternative loop that supported the results he wanted to see to support his growth in the Partner space.

Doug Silsbee referred to the loop that offers this alternative as the self-generative loop.[4]

The self-generative loop enables you to upgrade your identity to produce new results under a new performance framework; it represents a breakthrough for your growth. To access it, you need to intervene at the inner level of your responses, which hold in place your habits and identity.

The habits you've learnt behaviourally are engrained mentally, emotionally and somatically in your system.[5] To effectively break out of this in-built habit loop and explore self-generative behaviours, you need to intervene at these three levels. Intervening in one of them alters the others because they're interlinked.

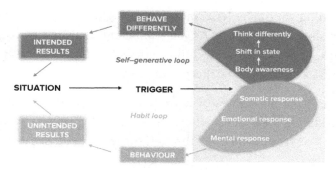

There are two approaches we will explore to catalyse and maximize the transformation across these three levels:

i. One is to intervene at the mental level and challenge your thinking so that you think differently.
ii. The other is to leverage on your body awareness to shift your mental and emotional state.

First approach: challenge your thinking by dancing between box and breakthrough stories

Intervening at the mental level involves altering the lens through which you interpret a situation, as well as the stories of interpretation that emerge because of it.

When you think differently about a situation, you start seeing new possibilities to behave differently that lead to new results. This means that you start challenging the edges of your box and dismantling your habit loop.

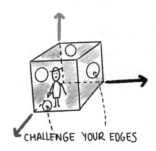

CHALLENGE YOUR EDGES

Dismantling your habit loop and considering new ways of behaving happen almost like a dance. As you realize and challenge the edges of your box, your identity and winning strategies, you start seeing new possibilities in how you're interpreting a situation.

This breakthrough moves you from being trapped in your box to considering new alternatives. When this happens, you dance between box stories and breakthrough stories to make sense of your experience.

Box stories often emerge as disempowering, unworried or limiting views of reality, capping or stagnating your growth and what you're trying to achieve. Breakthrough stories are those of personal growth, self-renewal, transformation and self-generation that enable you to consider new possibilities.[6]

Box stories

When leaders are trapped in a box story, they construct narratives about their situation where they believe there's no possibility for change, perpetuating their unintended results. This can limit their ability to achieve different outcomes and reinforce a sense of stagnation, as they often attribute their challenges to factors out of their control.

For example, box stories manifest in the following dialogue and thinking: their teams are not stepping up into their leadership, their peers don't promote change, the culture doesn't promote collaboration, the market is in recession, their calendars are packed, their management don't sponsor their cases for promotion… and so it continues.

When you engage in these types of stories, you build a perfect case that supports your current unintended results, almost justifying them, perpetuating a situation that you want to change, thereby trapping you in a box.

Breakthrough stories set you free from this.

Breakthrough stories

Breakthrough stories are empowering stories that enable you to see the situation differently and grow beyond the edges of your box. They emerge when you challenge your thinking and put a crack in your story of interpretation of a situation. Only then are you able to shift your focus to other elements of your context, yourself and others that you did not see before and reveal new possibilities to catalyse change, upgrade your identity and elevate your results.

As leaders engage in breakthrough stories, they see new untapped possibilities in the market to explore, they elicit new strategies to engage their team members so that they take on more responsibilities, they assess their stakeholders strategically to influence them or they re-structure their meetings to rise above the busyness of their calendars. These are just a few examples that we will explore in detail throughout the book to help you consider new leadership strategies.

You engage in a breakthrough story that reveals new possibilities once you have surfaced and challenged your box stories and understood how they were limiting you. That's why it's a dance.

Your identity can convince you that you are disempowered and limited about possibilities of change, trapping you in a box. But your freedom out of it is one insight away if you challenge your thinking by shifting your focus to other elements within the context.

The questions in the book are designed specifically for this; intended to help you gain new perspectives to lead your business, yourself and others differently.

> We left David's story at the point when he realized that he linked competence with his winning strategies of being operational, technical and tactical in client delivery. Transitioning to Partner, he needed to break out of his box, frame his role and sense of competence within a new universe of projects with new metrics to measure success and define the part he would play to make a difference.

By challenging his thinking, David shifted his focus from client delivery and technicalities to more strategic projects such as assessing market trends to upgrade services, exploring untapped cross-vertical opportunities and optimizing inter-vertical relationships and operations. This shift allowed him to think differently about how he could demonstrate his competence by mapping how his talents, team and connections could contribute to these projects.

From this place of renewed clarity, he engaged in 'breakthrough stories'. He identified what he needed to do differently for his next peer meeting: he wanted to present a case to suggest creating a transversal service offering across three internal divisions. For this he needed to reach out to the team leaders in each vertical and reorganize responsibilities within his team so that he could create space for strategic thinking in his calendar to put the case together.

Because your inner experience is interlinked across mind, emotions and body, changing your interpretation of the situation also alters the personal significance you give to it, thereby shifting your emotional state. Considering new possibilities enables you to access more resourceful and creative states that prompt you to take new actions.

Engaging in new stories of interpretation that lead to generative behaviours and upgrading your identity is just one insight away. But to maximize your insights, you need more than just powerful questions that challenge your thinking; you need to be in a state where you can look at the situation with clarity to see new possibilities.

Second approach: leverage on your body awareness

Powerful and quality insights are best generated in a state of calm and sharpened focus and awareness from where you can gain clarity about the situation.

Accessing these states can be challenging for leaders when they are trapped in their hectic calendars. Their accelerated rhythms can result in a mental clutter and emotional turmoil that prevent them from accessing a state from which they can generate new insights. This mental and emotional activity is deeply ingrained in their inner systems at a body level, making it more difficult to break free from this cycle of internal agitation and achieve states of calmness and sharpened focus.

Over time, any system may accumulate inefficiencies or errors that can hinder performance, and your inner system is no exception. If you want to access states that enable you to maximize the quality of your insights, you need to reset your inner system.

In the interlinked system of body, emotions and mind, a powerful way to reset your system is by intervening at the body level by leveraging your body awareness. You can do this by bringing attention to your breath, scanning your body or noticing body sensations.

The power of connecting with your body is its objectivity in this interlinked system of body, emotions and mind. Mental and emotional interpretations are biased by your own experience – the interpretation that you make of a situation and the personal significance you attach to it. However, your breath and body sensations are a tangible, physical experience that cuts through the hectic activity and subjectivity of your mind and emotions.

Shifting the focus out of your mind and into your body resets your inner system. By doing this, you provide stability to your mental and emotional states, enabling you to look at a situation with a calmer mind and enhanced awareness, thus promoting and supporting your transformation to generate new insights.

Strategically thinking about a situation might not translate into powerful insights if you're not in a mental and emotional state that supports this. Sometimes, merely taking perspective about a situation by going into the fishbowl is not enough to have a breakthrough.

Imagine that you're polluted with toxicity from the ocean waters. If you don't rinse before going into the fishbowl, you'll bring that toxicity into it and you won't be swimming in clean water from where you can see things clearly.

To maximize the quality of the insights and gain renewed clarity, you need to reset your inner system from the accumulated inefficiencies and mental clutter and emotions that can be engrained in your body from dealing with multiple situations in your day-to-day activities.

In this link (https://www.insatiable-leaders.com/book-bonus) you'll find a 5-minute audio. It's a breathing and body scan exercise to help you reset your mental and emotional state, think more clearly and generate new insights. We'll also come back to it in the last section of the book, meta-abilities, when we delve into the importance of developing presence.

By developing your body awareness, you extend this heightened mindfulness to become aware of new possibilities within your context. This enables you to lead more consciously in your day-to-day situations.

~

The two approaches explored in this section will enable you to raise your game and upgrade your identity in critical situations for your growth by challenging your thinking and accessing calmer states. With a renewed sense of possibilities and from more resourceful and creative states, you become readier and better equipped to take new actions.

However, your job with your old identity is not done; it will try to pull you back into old ways of thinking and behaving.

Step 4: Reinforce your new identity

As leaders endeavour to adopt new behaviours to lead their business, themselves and their teams differently, they might encounter friction within their environment. This friction can stem from their own discomfort or unfamiliarity with new behaviours or others' resistance to change.

For example, as David considered restructuring his calendar, reassigning responsibilities within his team and manoeuvring the political chessboard, he would notice resistance when he needed to say no to meetings or when he needed to reach out to new stakeholders he had not established a connection with. This tension or potential discomfort could lead him to revert to old behaviours and habits, blocking his identity upgrade.

When you behave in new ways, you are stepping away from the comfort and familiarity of your habits and the perception that others have of you based on how you behave with them. Your old identity doesn't like funky and unfamiliar experiments nor experiencing discomfort, which is why it may resist change.

The system of attachments and aversions under which your identity operates has aversion towards situations that are not familiar or hold as difficult or challenging. This means that when you seek to adopt new behaviours, your old identity will try to pull you back to old ways of behaving. While these are familiar for you and others, you're blocking your identity upgrade.

To counterbalance this pattern, you need to have a force that pulls you out of that trap in the opposite direction. That force is your vision: the stand you take, which we explored in the previous pillar 'Elevate your vision'.

As such, there are two forces pulling in opposite directions as you seek to adopt different behaviours that support new and intended results: your old identity versus your stand.

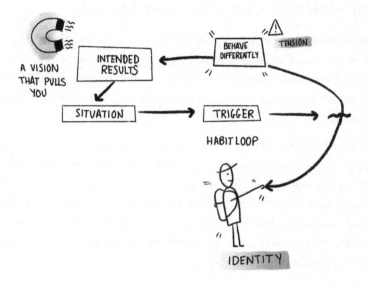

Being connected to your vision in the context of your inner transformation acts like a magnet that pulls you out of the temptation of your old identity where you would revert to your habit loop in the face of obstacles, resistance and discomfort.

"Remind me what you're after. Remind me why it's worth it for you and why it's worth it for others." This is what I would ask David as he encountered friction, was blocked by obstacles or did not achieve the responses from his teams and peers that he wished. It enabled him to connect with his bigger vision, his case for Partner and what was at the other side of the obstacles and resistance if he transcended the tension. It reconnected him with his aspirations and the growth possibilities for his team members, clients and peers in his division.

Connecting to your stand connects you to growth possibilities both for you and the environment you seek to engage. You connect with the impact you can make in the industry, how your teams can grow within this new space and the difference it can make to the organization.

From this stand and vision that you declare from the future, you can see new possibilities beyond the resistance to elicit new strategies to overcome obstacles, give meaning to your transformation and influence your environment in the frame of this new vision.

Your stand frames your individual transformation, calling you to grow beyond the edges of your box. That's why it's critical for leaders to frame their leadership development in the context of a vision that stretches and inspires them and to which they're connected. That's why before delving into this current pillar 'Elevate your identity', you first need to tackle the pillar 'Elevate your vision'.

Making leadership development merely about upskilling or tackling competencies without linking it to a vision that stretches you and calls you to transform can reduce the degree of efficiency and sustainability of your behavioural upgrade to produce elevated results. This is why this last fourth step to elevate your identity is critical.

The 4Rs for your ongoing identity elevation

The last sections have guided you through four steps to break out of your box and upgrade your identity to elevate your results under a stretched framework. They consolidate into a 4R process illustrated below: recognition, realization, reframing and reinforcement.

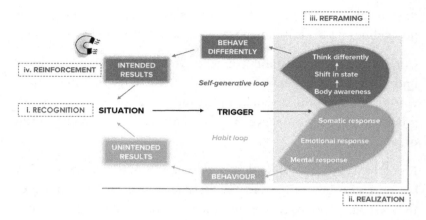

i. **Recognition**: identify the critical situations for your growth in which you are not producing the results that support your vision or objectives.

ii. **Realization**: gain awareness about how your identity and habits are keeping you in a box, surfacing your identity's attachments and aversions and winning strategies.

iii. **Reframing**: intervene at the inner level to reframe your story and gain new insights by leveraging your body awareness.

iv. **Reinforcement**: counterbalance the tension of behaving in new ways, anchoring yourself in your stand and vision.

These are the 4Rs that will enable you to upgrade your identity in a situation where you want to break out of your box and elevate your results in the frame of your pioneer vision and stretched objectives.

To achieve effective inner transformation and sustain it, it's crucial to intervene at the identity level, surfacing the attachments and aversions that are the crux of your development, and frame your growth within a bigger cause that you align with personally. Only then will you be pulled out of your box and old habits to upgrade your identity and create new results.

However, this identity upgrade has an expiry date.

4Rs ^{n}: become a self-generative leader

The reason why the upgraded identity has an expiry date is because of the complexity of the system leaders operate in, with increasingly complex demands they need to tackle and their own insatiable drive to grow that propels them to reach the next threshold.

The truth is that there will come a time when that newly upgraded identity will become obsolete. This will happen when it no longer supports the results you seek to create in situations where something different is required from you. This means that you'll end up in a (new) box, and you will need to engage in the 4R process again.

Each new challenge and aspiration will require something different from you, and you will need a new identity to generate those results. You'll need to become a new leader. At each moment in time, you will need to break out of your box and default habits and continuously explore new self-generative ways to show up in more demanding and complex situations. You need to become a self-generative leader who continuously upgrades to a new identity that supports each challenge and new vision.[7]

To become a self-generative leader, you need to master your capacity to break out of boxes repeatedly, engaging into the 4R process each time as if you elevated it to the nth power. This is what fuels limitless growth and enables you to drive meaningful transformation continuously.

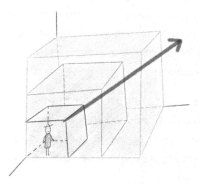

The purpose of becoming a self-generative leader is to move beyond an identity that no longer serves you towards new ways of being, thinking and behaving that aligns with your increasingly stretched visions and objectives.

Fernando Flores notes: 'You have to be able to risk your identity for a bigger future than the present you're living.'

Becoming self-generative is a choice that requires you to add intentionality into your developmental journey, constantly upgrading your identity to reach higher aspirations. Failing to do so may result in falling short of your desired results, impact and momentum.

To become a self-generative leader, you need to engage the process of the 4Rs repeatedly. The questions at the end of the chapter will provide guidance for this.

Fundamentals

- Your **identity and habits** you have learned to engage in keep you in a box, which are held in place by a system of *attachments and aversions.*

- Upon a *trigger*, you **respond** *somatically* (a conditioned response in your body), *emotionally* (based on your deep story that determines the quality of your state) and *mentally* (based on your interpretation). These internal responses result in *behaviour.*

- When you engage in similar responses, you default into a **habit loop** that can lead to *unintended results*, if they are not aligned with your vision and objectives. Your **winning strategies** play a critical role in keeping you trapped in this loop. But there is hope!

- The **self-generative loop** leads to resourceful and creative ways of responding to upgrade your identity. To access it, you need to intervene at the inner level, which is the crux of your development. There are two approaches to help you with this:

    i. Challenge your thinking to move from a box story to a breakthrough story.

    ii. Leverage your body awareness to shift your mental and emotional state and improve the quality of your insights.

- To reinforce your identity upgrade and avoid reverting to old habits, you need to anchor yourself in your stand to hold and transcend the **tension** and engage your environment.

- The above steps entail a **4R-step** process:

    i. Recognize the situation.

    ii. Realize your habit loop.

    iii. Reframe your inner responses to access the self-generative loop.

    iv. Reinforce your identity upgrade.

- Each new challenge and aspiration will require something different from you, and you'll need to engage in the 4R-step process repeatedly to upgrade your identity upon each new challenge. This requires you to become a **self-generative leader**.

Into the fishbowl: bring intentionality to your development

Consider the following questions for situations in which you would like to elevate your results. While you might need questions specific to your situation to explore it in more detail, these can help you gain a new level of awareness to start considering new possibilities.

If your situation relates to team, culture, political chessboard or time, you might find insights to support your transformation in the next chapters.

For the purpose of the exercise, the 4Rs are not in order.

1. **Recognize:** in which situation would you like to create different results?

2. **Realize:** why are you not achieving them? What's the barrier you perceive, and how do you *explain* it? Be as specific as you can so that you can identify what's triggering you.

3. **Realize:** what action do you take as a result? In which way does it lead to *unintended results*?

4. **Reinforce:** what are the results you like to achieve instead? Why would achieving them make a difference to you, your business and others in your environment?

5. **Reframe:** who is creating the results you want to see? Who are they *being* and how are they *behaving* in ways you are not? Where is their *focus/thinking* to behave this way?

Chapter 5

Elevate your environment

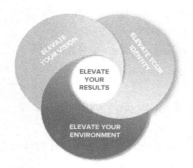

This chapter looks into how to stretch the thinking of players in your environment and hone the conditions to support your growth and transformation.

I refer to the environment as the conditions and organizational system under which you operate.

Your environment sets your performance. (Period.)

Your capacity to upgrade it and reinforce it will fuel and catalyse your transformation, injecting momentum to drive impact and next-level performance at scale.

In this chapter, we will explore three strategies to achieve this:

i.   Foster a team of A-players to cultivate autonomy and increased performance.
ii. Create units of excellence in the groups you operate (high-performing teams and micro-cultures).
iii. Master the political chessboard to drive change at scale.

By the end of this chapter, you'll:

- learn the mental shift required to catalyse growth in a complex environment.
- explore the pitfalls that block you from creating next-level results with your direct reports, teams, peer groups and the stakeholders you seek to engage.
- discover micro-interactions and manoeuvres to upgrade the interactions you have with them to support your aspirations.

Become a catalyst of the environment: the paradox to upgrade it

> 'You don't raise to the level of your goals,
> you fall to the level of your systems.'
>
> *James Clear*
>
> **To Sushant**

Sushant instilled the insatiable essence all compressed within him. His mind was in the future, always switched on to take on the next challenge ahead of him to propel his career and team forward.

He was always looking for strategies to stretch himself, challenge his developmental edges and break out of his box. And he sought to extend this mindset to others in his environment.

He was the Vice President of a technology solutions provider in the UK & Ireland. He wanted to instil this continuous improvement mentality amongst his team peers and stakeholders, seeking to stretch their thinking to perform in more demanding circumstances and to engage them in his efforts to foster innovation internally.

However, his strategies to stretch and mobilize others did not translate into the results, buy-in and engagement he sought. Nor did they achieve the degree, speed and level of progress he was looking for.

He attributed the obstacles to external factors such as cultural barriers, internal politics and people's mentalities and appetite for change different to his. What he did not see is that this way of thinking prevented him from owning his part and exploring alternative leadership strategies to upgrade the culture, lead his team members to reach their next level of potential, foster agility in his division and challenge others' thinking to engage them in change.

While his self-reliance enabled him to make progress and achieve higher results, if he didn't intervene in his environment and upgrade the condition under which he operated, he would be at their mercy, and they would determine, and sometimes cap, his individual, team and company growth.

To change this, he needed to become a catalyst of the environment.

Victim vs catalyst of the environment

The environment is the conditions and organizational system under which you operate. The environment of an organization encompasses a wide range of interrelated factors and components, including people, corporate culture, organizational structure and technological systems.

For transformation and growth to take place, there needs to be an environment that promotes them. Otherwise, growth and transformation will be limited, capped or slowed down.

Environment sets performance and it serves the framework to support your progression through growth thresholds. You can visualize it as a the 'container' which promotes growth at each stage of your journey. This implies that to operate at higher levels of demands, excellence and results, you'll need an upgraded version of the environment that fosters those aspirations. This means that as you elevate your vision, you need to elevate your environment to promote that growth.

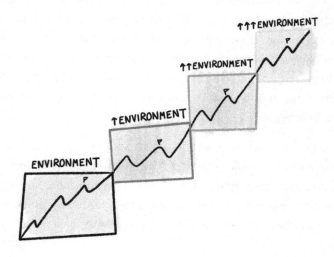

Upgrading the environment is catalytic for your growth for two reasons, illustrated in the drawing below: it's a propulsor and a catapult.

- **Propulsor**: stretching your team's capabilities, fostering agility, harnessing technology and engaging stakeholders in change fuels you to overcome obstacles to bring your vision further and injects velocity to your journey.
- **Catapult**: as you progress, you raise the standards, and the environment you've built has become a catapult from where you can reach the next growth threshold. Aiming for significantly new aspirations and objectives can only happen if you've built the foundations from where to keep growing.

As promising as it sounds, the environmental conditions don't always promote transformation.

Leaders seek to implement their visions and pursue their objectives, but they can face obstacles that can limit or slow down progress. These can include team underperformance, lack of coordination, misalignment, cultural barriers, operational inefficiency or people blocking change.

It's exactly those conditions that Sushant and other leaders need to intervene in and change if they want to propel their growth. However, this can be a more arduous and frustrating experience for leaders compared to advancing their individual journeys. For example, it did not require the same effort for Sushant to keep himself accountable for excellent results or progress towards his objectives as it did to inspire others to deliver extraordinary results or engage them in change. As a result, he started to view these obstacles as something difficult to influence and significantly change.

If you consider that the environment is set, difficult to change or dependent on others to change it, you become a victim of it and are at its mercy. This mindset is robbing you of the opportunity to become a catalyst of the environment and consider new strategies to upgrade it to support your aspirations.

To be a catalyst of the environment, you need to comprehend its systemic complexity.

The paradox to drive change in a complex system

The environment is a complex whole of diverse people, units, divisions and hidden rules interconnected between them. Effectively upgrading your environment requires you to have a helicopter view of the system to map these elements and assess their interrelation and causality in the context of the vision you lead.

Intervening in this complex system can appear as a difficult and time-consuming experience for leaders. However, upgrading the environment is often more feasible than they realize: you can catalyse change by harnessing the power of small manoeuvres and micro-interactions.

Transformation happens in intentional and strategic micro-interactions and manoeuvres in your day-to-day situations – one conversation at a time and one peer-to-peer meeting at a time. The paradox of environmental upgrade lies in introducing small alterations to drive a bigger transformation at a systemic level.

In the following sections, we will explore three environmental strategies to help you upgrade the environment through this lens: fostering a team of A-players, creating units of excellence and groups and mastering the political chessboard.

What will give you an edge in mastering these strategies is assessing your system with a helicopter view as you go into the fishbowl, enabling you to identify small manoeuvres to make strides in how you lead each team member, your team, your peer group and stakeholders on the political chessboard.

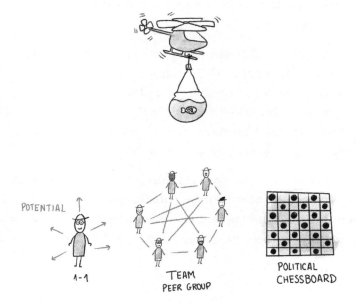

For each environmental strategy, you'll learn the common pitfalls and mental shifts required to optimize it, and you'll find an activity to reflect on each one of them separately.

Strategy 1: Foster a team of A-players

One of the biggest obstacles to deliver on a stretched or pioneer vision is a leadership lag, not only in you as a leader but also in your team members, who are the players who can make you deliver on that vision.

To solve this lag, you need to stretch your team members' abilities and mentalities to thrive and to lead under a stretched framework.

I consider a team of A-players a team with individuals that:

- deliver beyond their ordinary levels of performance.
- aim to achieve higher standards of contribution, quality and efficiency to drive individual and team advancement.
- make decisions on their own and take on more responsibilities because they've cultivated their autonomy and leadership criteria.

To get the most out of team players, team leaders need to have conversations to stretch their team members' capabilities and growth frameworks beyond their everyday responsibilities. Equally, it requires the team leader to explore the mindset and conditions impacting their team members' performance to intervene in them and upgrade them to set their team members' up for success.

Engaging in this process requires leaders to create a space with their team members to foster their own individual transformation. Still, many leaders miss this opportunity in their day-to-day conversations or don't create a space in their calendars for it. They make their one-to-one interactions about project status or technicalities, which don't always translate into the increased autonomy, leadership capabilities or performance they want and need from their team. This was Sushant's case.

To advance team members in their developmental journey, set them up for success and empower them to take on more responsibilities, Sushant needed to become a coach.

This strategy explores how leaders need to shift their focus in how they approach their one-to-ones, along with the model and identity required to coach their team members.

Beyond project status and technicalities: focus on individuals' transformation

In Sushant's endeavours to help his team succeed in acquiring new businesses and performing in more demanding circumstances, he regularly had one-to-one conversations with them. In these interactions, he would answer their questions, share tips and strategies to help them progress with projects and seek to develop them on the technical skills to perform at their job.

Although these exchanges did help his team to make progress with their day-to-day responsibilities, they inadvertently fostered an over-reliance on Sushant's guidance in situations where Sushant wanted them to step up in their leadership.

Sushant wanted his team members to make leaps in their thinking, become autonomous and be proactive to take on more responsibilities. This would allow him to free up his time to create more business opportunities which him and his team could grow in and focus on.

However, his team development approach was not translating into any of these intentions and results.

When it comes to the development of their team members, and specifically their direct reports, leaders tend to make their one-to-one interactions about 'catch-ups', updates on the project status or developing the technicalities for their job. While these conversations are critical for their team members' progression, they leave little focus to stretch their leadership capabilities and mindset and foster their leadership development.

If Sushant wanted his team members to operate under greater autonomy and take on more responsibilities, he needed to show up with a different focus in the one-to-one conversations. Instead of simply providing guidance and strategies, he needed to *draw out* his team members with thought-provoking questions.

Drawing out your team members involves prompting them into introspection and self-discovery, encouraging them to elicit their own answers, explore their own ideas and conclusions and take ownership of their growth journeys. The questions we'll explore in this section are designed for this.

They will enable your team members to see beyond their day-to-day tasks into more ambitious objectives, enhance their critical thinking, uncover the mentalities and conditions that promote or hinder their potential and foster autonomy in leading their day-to-day responsibilities.

To achieve these outcomes, instead of sharing strategies and answers, which might be quicker, easier or which you might consider helpful for their growth, you need to ask questions to elicit their views. The image on the next page illustrates how you transition from conversations where you provide inputs, to conversations where they provide inputs to you.

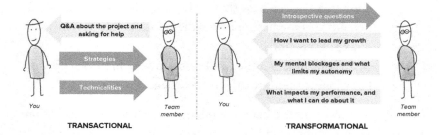

When you interact with your team members through the transformational lens, you move from the transactional conversations that enable them to make incremental steps in their day-to-day projects into conversations that require them to shift their focus and gain awareness about new elements in their context and themselves. When this happens, there is an alteration in their thinking that fosters their internal transformation, simultaneously enabling you and them to uncover the conditions that need to be in place for them to experience success.

Engaging in these conversations requires you to foster a space for their transformation. You need to become a coach in your one-on-one interactions.

Become a coach: a model and an identity

Coaching requires you to create a space for transformation in your one-to-one interactions with your team members to actively help them gain new insights about their role, themselves and how they interact with others to achieve next-level results.

By engaging with your team members this way you can:

- empower them to raise their aspirations and ownership about their career and leadership development, increasing their engagement in their day-to-day activities.

- guide them to see how they operate in situations that block their advancement, supporting them to generate new insights to take new actions.
- explore and enhance the conditions under which they operate that support their growth and set them up for success.

Each one of these points tackles the pillars of the leadership elevation model – vision, identity and environment (conditions). You can use this as a model to foster their development by drawing them out around these critical aspects for their growth.

Let's explore how this model can guide you in your one-to-one interactions and then the identity you need to embrace to maximize its potential.

A model: draw your team members out across the three pillars

Here's the model you can use to become a coach and foster your teams' development to elevate *their* vision, elevate *their* leadership and elevate *their* conditions.

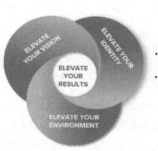

- Co-create a vision that pulls them
- Stretch their developmental framework

ELEVATE YOUR VISION

ELEVATE YOUR IDENTITY

ELEVATE YOUR RESULTS

ELEVATE YOUR ENVIRONMENT

- Explore situations in which they feel limited or blocked
- Stretch their mindset in how they're thinking about a situation

- Set them up for success by upgrading how we operate and are set up as a team

Sushant's journey will help us illustrate how leaders can play a part in helping team members to grow in each pillar.

I. Elevate their vision

"I want my team members to play a bigger game and set themselves for higher results," Sushant confessed.

"Then, you need to start by raising the aspirations and growth objectives they're aiming for," I replied.

"How do I do that?"

"You need to shape a framework in which they can think bigger than their current day-to-day responsibilities."

Elevating their vision involves engaging with your team members to co-create a stretched framework for their development. This is a framework in which they can grow and stretch their contribution, maximize their ideas and talents, rise above the day-to-day activities and gain a new perspective on their roles and what they can achieve.

The key lies in stretching their aspirations and exploring areas in which they would like to grow in the context of organizational needs.

You can use these questions with them:

1. What are the untapped *problems or opportunities* you observe in our industry or with our clients that we're not addressing?
2. What's *missing* in how we're operating as a team that prevents us from tackling them?
3. Which *two solutions* would you propose to tackle them?
4. What are *three achievements* you would like to celebrate by the end of the month? Or, where would you want to have led your clients, results and projects by the end of the month?
5. What's the *one contribution* you would have liked to make in the team by the end of this month?
6. What's the *one change* you need to introduce in how you operate to tackle those aspirations?
7. If you could only *ask me one question* to support you in tackling those aspirations, what would it be and why?

Asking these questions once a month or every quarter to your direct reports enables you to co-create a stretched framework for them to grow into that they have drawn from within and taken ownership of. This contributes to increasing their engagement to pursue it.

The focus here aligns with what you explored in the 'Elevate your vision' pillar, but now we're tailoring it to their specific circumstances. In other words, you help them create a *pull vision* that fuels them beyond obstacles and day-to-day activities, enabling them to expand their potential and the space of possibilities and putting their day-to-day actions into the context of a more significant vision they align to personally because they've drawn from within.

II. Elevate their identity

Like you, your team members are in boxes too at any given moment. Elevating their identity involves helping them to challenge the developmental edges of their boxes to elevate their performance and overcome more demanding obstacles in their day-to-day commitments and aspirations. However, Sushant's focus was somewhere else.

"I want my team to be more confident and equipped pitching to potential clients at C-Level," Sushant shared, "but they end up being stuck and I need to jump in and intervene. I would like them to develop the mindset to succeed independently."

"Sushant, if you want your team to overcome their blockages on their own, they need to understand how they're tripping over developmental edges and reach their own conclusions to overcome these challenges. To foster their autonomy and leadership, your focus should be directed to guide them in this process, not just giving them the answers. You need to help them break out of their box."

To foster a team of A-players, every leader needs to understand that their team members' identities lead them to default into similar ways of thinking and behaving in situations in their day-to-day activities, trapping them in a box. If you want your team members to make leaps in the results they create and their capabilities, you need to help them challenge the edges of that box.

With questions, you can guide them to understand how they reach a limit and how they interpret it to shift their focus and make them think about their problems from a different angle and consider other possibilities for advancement in critical situations for their growth.

Often we fail to overcome challenges because we haven't fully considered what's necessary for growth, and we have not sketched out the problem from all the angles. The questions in the list below will help your team members gain new perspectives and will help you reveal their inner blockages to help them more impactfully.

1. In which *situation* do you feel limited or blocked? In which situation would you like to double your performance?
2. What has been *accomplished*? That is, what have you done to lead you to the current level of success and why has it worked out?
3. Where are you *blocked*? What have you tried and why is it not working?
4. What does *success* look like once you've succeeded in this situation?

5. What are *two questions* you have that, if they got answered, would turn this situation around? Why those two?
6. What's *missing* that, if provided, would make the difference to turn this situation around?
7. Why is that not in place *yet*?

These questions go beyond the technical aspects of their job, aiming to explore how they perceive situations and their approach to them. They provide insight into how they handle challenges as they progress with their responsibilities and foster their ability to start identifying the path to new possibilities and solutions.

The work with these questions is first done on their side, rather than on yours, as you might be tempted to jump in to help them, as Sushant did. Coaching your team members requires you to create a space for them to draw the answers on their own and for this you need to hold back from leaning into the solution. It's in that space where an alteration in their thinking can take place.

Instead of giving them answers, strategies or sharing your own views, you need to unpack and challenge their thinking first to let them gain a more strategic understanding about the problem and their leadership.

As Eugène Ionesco said: 'It is not the answer that enlightens, but the question.'

By asking powerful questions, you stretch their focus and raise the level of the conversation to a new level of thinking that they were not accessing before. Only then can they start to see different possibilities, reaching new answers on their own and asking you more powerful questions to lever their growth.

III. Elevate their conditions

Elevating their conditions requires you to identify the settings in your team environment that limit or propel your team members' growth and upgrade those, enabling them to maximize the success they can experience at an individual and team level to achieve their objectives.

This involves understanding inefficiencies, blockages or catalysts for growth in how you operate in the team and how you're set up. It is about, for example, understanding inefficiencies in coordination, team alignment, team ownership, processes and resource allocation. Equally, it is about surfacing potential conflicts or dynamics in the team that impact their performance.

Instead of running climate surveys or perpetuating inefficient conditions, you can harness the power of micro-interactions with your team to identify and address the critical conditions that unlock blockages in their day-to-day performance.

The intention of this manoeuvre is not to debate or complain about the culture. Instead, the focus is on action; on guiding them to identify a critical condition impacting their performance that they can change in the next team interaction by introducing small adjustments they can take ownership for and you support them with.

To succeed in elevating the conditions by performing small manoeuvres, Sushant needed two allies: focus and partnership:

- **Narrowing their focus** helps you and your team members to identify the critical conditions out of many that will make the biggest difference to their performance. This enables both of you to channel your intentions and energy to upgrade those.
- **Building a partnership** involves drawing from them a specific, small action they commit to take, where you can be part of the solution to support their choice.

Leveraging these allies enables you to increase your team members' accountability to take action and shift their mindset from a complaining lens to an accountability lens.

The following questions will help you guide your team members to introduce small adjustments in the team conditions to advance with their objectives.

1. What are *three factors* of how we're set up and operating as a team that promote your success, your performance or your progress with [this objective]?
2. What are *three factors or conditions* that are hindering your success, negatively impacting your performance or making you ineffective?
3. What's the *one thing* that needs to change to double your performance? (Ally: focus on a critical condition.)
4. What's *one thing* you need to do differently to drive this change? What's *one thing* you need from me? (Ally: partnership.)

The next section, 'Create units of excellence', explores how these changes can lead to cultural upgrades in the team as a group.

But before getting there, let's delve into the identity you need to embrace as a coach to maximize the potential of this three-pillar coaching model.

Upgrade your identity

Fostering a team of A-players is about assessing and exploring what would bring each individual to their 'A-est' version at each stage in their journey and build a case for their development. There might be some players that operate at higher levels of impact, performance and leadership in comparison to others, but you can stretch each individual's potential to their next level if you set yourself that intention and believe that you're the catalyst for each individual's growth.

To succeed in this, you need to build a case for development for each individual in your team or direct report. This requires you to step back and assess this person from a distance, observing how they operate, seeing beyond their limitations and current level of performance and excellence, and exploring how things can be arranged to help that person experience success.

As you take perspective and build a case for development, you can show up strategically and intentionally in the one-to-one interactions to coach them.

Coaching your team members requires you to create a space for their transformation. This means that you need to frame the one-to-one conversations differently to draw them out with questions, rather than jumping in with solutions, answers or technicalities.

You don't need to lead all your one-to-ones with a coaching hat, as there are moments where the conversation needs to be about project status or technicalities. However, making a space for coaching conversations once or twice a month with your direct reports will enable them to make leaps in their thinking, leadership and autonomy.

Coaching your team members does not require so much a shift in your calendar to make time for it, but rather a shift in your mindset, in your identity; it's about how you're showing up to the conversation and harnessing the power of micro-interactions. What's more, as your team members grow in autonomy and critical thinking as a result of coaching, you can streamline your team structure and delegate confidently, assigning responsibilities and freeing up your calendar to pursue new strategic opportunities.

Let's look at an activity that you can do to assess your team members to build a case for their development.

Become a coach: assess your team members to build a case for their development

Assess each one of your team members or direct reports before your next one-to-one to prepare for your coaching conversation.

Assess

Vision:

1. From 1–10, at which level of *potential* is this person operating, 10 being the highest?
2. What would get them to 9/10?
3. What's the latent potential I see in this person that I want to unlock? For example, ideas they can implement, talents they can exploit, where they can step up more in their leadership, in team interventions or projects, etc.

Identity:

1. From 1–10, how would I rate this person's *performance* over the last two weeks?
2. What's holding them back from a higher level of performance and leadership?

Conditions:

Considering how we're set up and operating as a team, which *three conditions* limit this person's performance and contribution?

Prepare for your coaching conversation

Review the questions shared for each pillar of the model: elevate their vision, elevate their leadership, elevate their conditions. With this in mind, consider, based on this assessment:

- Which *three* questions can I ask this person in my next coaching conversation to elicit their thinking and stretch their potential?

To foster a team of A-players you need to recognize and nurture the uniqueness, aspirations and drivers of your team members and cultivate an environment in which they can thrive. Let's now explore how to foster a high-performing environment.

Strategy 2: Create units of excellence: high-performing teams and micro-cultures

I refer to units as the organizational structures under which people in a company are organized with a shared area of focus, objectives and ambitions. Examples of units are teams, divisions, peer groups, boards and even the whole company itself as an 'organism'.

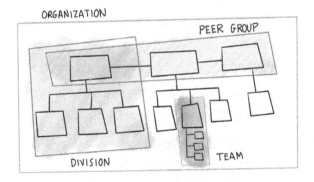

Under those units, people operate in groups.

Group interactions are the spaces of possibilities where people's ideas, experiences, talents and energy come together to create something new and lead units and companies to new spaces.

The quality of the group interactions determines the dialogues people engage in to foster new thinking, the performance standards to drive results and the efficiency at which they're achieved. They either drive or hinder innovation, diversity, performance, excellence and agility.

Some leaders, including Sushant, sometimes consider that the conditions and dynamics that govern the units under which they operate depend on the organizational culture. As a result, they might feel they that they lack power or capacity to enact significant change to upgrade them in a way that would promote advancement within the unit, perpetuating ways of operating that can cap excellence, transformation and momentum.

The purpose of this strategy is to awaken leaders' commitment to create units of excellence where the interactions of its members and the conditions under which they operate are such that individuals can do the most innovative and robust thinking together. These are units where people in the group share and challenge ideas and foster agility, and where transformative initiatives and exceptional results become the norm.

This section explores how you can become the catalyser of that upgrade in the units you belong to by intervening in the group day-to-day interactions.

Don't expect a top-down approach, catalyse a bottom-up change

Groups have the potential to amplify new ideas and performance when they harness the talents, perspectives and capabilities of their members. However, they also can introduce a source of complexity and challenge in organizational dynamics.

Operating within groups introduces complexities related to communication, coordination and alignment of goals and priorities. Additionally, it involves managing polarizing views, biases, blurred accountability and interpersonal dynamics such as power struggles, lack of trust or conflicting agendas.

These inefficiencies limit innovation, hinder performance and block momentum, and they can overwhelm, frustrate or demotivate leaders as they seek to roll up their sleeves and instigate change within their groups.

While Sushant wanted to solve the inefficiencies he encountered in his teams and peer groups, he also portrayed a sense of powerlessness to intervene in them. Amidst his day-to-day responsibilities and the complexity that these group challenges revealed, he inferred the reason of such inefficacies was culture.

It was not an unfounded assumption after all. Elements such as values, norms, collaboration methods, decision-making processes, knowledge sharing and accountability are deeply influenced by the overarching company culture.

But attributing this problem solely to culture was preventing him from rising above these inefficiencies and upgrading his day-to-day team interactions to foster growth and transformation.

Some leaders think that they will overcome these group inefficiencies and complexities when there is a cultural change that comes from top management (a top-down approach) or when others take a lead to change them. This kind of thinking positions them as victims of these conditions and perpetuates, and even aggravates, the inefficiencies.

To rise above these traps, they need to reassess how they look at culture, because only then can they re-evaluate their capacity to catalyse change in the groups they lead.

Company culture and conditions work at a complex and macro level in an organization – across individuals, divisions, teams and countries. Being trapped in this complexity can make leaders depend on a top-down intervention, preventing them from thinking about culture and conditions in practical terms in their day-to-day interactions.

When leaders start to look at culture through the lens of the behaviours, standards and conversations they nurture, reinforce or disregard within their teams or peer groups, they have the key to upgrade them.

The point of this shift is not to disregard the complexity of what company culture and cultural change entail. Instead, it's to awaken leaders' capacity to enact change by intervening through micro-interactions in their groups, thereby raising the level of the conversations and standards and driving momentum. When they do this, they take ownership of the units they are part of and spark change from the bottom up into the system. Instead of feeling trapped and limited by culture, which they consider as unchangeable and out of their control, they take ownership to elevate the groups they can influence.

To embrace this shift, you need to assess and gain new insights into those day-to-day group interactions you can upgrade. This requires understanding the intricacies of how your group operates.

Elevate your group identity

In the same way you have an identity, so does the group you belong to. Similarly, just as you engage in practised behaviours and ways of thinking, you do so in your groups as well, with conversations you nurture or avoid or ways of interacting that you're familiar with.

This is not inherently good or bad, but it's limiting for group advancement and fostering innovation.

While group interactions are opportunities to create something new to lead units and the company to new spaces, group identity gets in the way of this. It can lead the group to engage in inefficient patterns and ways of thinking that do not foster conversations and interactions that would advance your unit and promote collaboration and fresh thinking.

This means that your group identity traps your group in a box, capping the collective intelligence, performance and vitality of the group to produce higher-level results at scale.

The good news is that in the same way you can upgrade your identity, you can upgrade your group identity if you intervene at its core.

What holds your group identity in place is the dialogues and dynamics you engage in. The dialogues are what you speak about and where your focus is during the conversation, and the dynamics reveal how you interact, behave and engage in conversations.

As you engage in default group dialogues and dynamics, you risk ending up in a box that can cap how your unit interacts and performs – whether it's your team, peer group or your board.

To change that, you need to intervene in the default patterns and engage in robust dialogues and catalytic dynamics to create something new and break out of your 'group box'.

D²: elevate the dialogues and dynamics

Dialogues and dynamics are the keys to leading your group into something new in each micro-interaction or meeting.

Dialogues are the doorways to people's focus, to their thinking. They come to the surface through the language they use in the group.

Dynamics result from how each person shows up and behaves in the group and how they interact with each other and between each other.

To upgrade your group identity and elevate your interactions, you first need to assess the inefficient dialogues and dynamics that are hindering your group performance. Then you need to lean in intentionally in the next meeting to upgrade the group identity by harnessing the power of micro-interactions.

Assess

Assessing your group is about stepping back and observing the people, their dialogues and the interaction from a distance. You need to gain a helicopter view of:

- how each participant is thinking, which is revealed in their dialogues, as well as how they behave and show up in the group, which will enable you to gain insights into the group dynamics.
- the effect or impact that each individual's dialogue and behaviour triggers in an individual within the group or at the group level.
- how each individual's intervention (or lack thereof) either enhances or hinders your group's performance, cohesion, momentum and results.

Gaining a helicopter view of your group enables you to observe how your team members or peers operate together and with you. This is about assessing for example who is speaking and who is not; what's the impact in the conversation when someone intervenes or not; what or who is slowing down decision making, etc.

The focus is to identify inefficient dialogues and dynamics that can cap transformation, performance standards and momentum in groups.

Below, you'll find some examples of this. I invite you to connect with how they manifest in your team, peer groups or boards before going into your fishbowl.

- Some individuals within the group hold back from sharing ideas and perspectives or challenging others, thereby capping the flow of different perspectives that enrich the group and perpetuating the status quo.
- There are some 'supermen or superwomen' that seek to solve problems on their own. According to Margaret Heffernan, this takes place when some organizations, or units, run according to 'the super chicken model', where the value is placed on star employees who outperform others, preventing the group from doing their best thinking together.[1]
- Some players protect their status and aren't open to challenge.
- There is a low level of positive or constructive conflict in establishing the objectives and raising the aspirations of the unit.
- There are undiscussable matters that drain the energy, disengage and decrease the focus of everyone involved. These can be things such as unsolved matters, past or overlooked conflicts, defensiveness, unkept agreements, or unmet performance or deadlines by someone in the group.
- Some players engage in complaints that do not advance the system instead of proposing initiatives and ideas to encourage change along with a plan for action.
- There are ideas for transformation that are left in the air or the backburner, without landing them in plans or designating clear accountability.

With these examples in mind, I invite you to consider the following activity to assess a group interaction you want to elevate with a team, peer group or board.

Assess and elevate your group identity

Reflect about a team or peer meeting that you would like to upgrade.

1. From 1–10, how would I rate the *competitiveness* of my unit (team or peer group)?
2. What's the *key* dialogue or dynamic holding us back the most from a bigger level of competitiveness?
3. What are the *two* dialogues that would enable my unit to experience a higher degree of competitiveness and success and/or will drive advancement?
4. What are the *two* dynamics that would enable my unit to experience a higher degree of competitiveness and success and/or will drive advancement?
5. What is the *one* dialogue or dynamic I need to nurture/ welcome/stop in my next interaction to double the momentum and growth of my unit?

Lean in one shift at a time

The idea from those questions is that you gain new insights and identify a small step you can take in a new direction in the next group meeting to shift the dynamics and dialogues.

Sushant realized that each individual in his team faced obstacles gaining new clients and pitching, however they were not sharing them in the team as a group. As a result, they could not benefit from other strategies that their teammates had applied in similar situations.

Sushant saw an opportunity to leverage the group's intelligence, ideas, experience, expertise and diversity to gain traction in advancing the group as a whole. He decided to change the set-up in some team meetings to explore these obstacles as a group.

It was a space where each individual would share where they were blocked and the rest of the group would challenge ideas and share success strategies to overcome obstacles and elevate sales strategies and practices.

These questions are designed with a bias towards action and small manoeuvres such as the one Sushant took. Make this process organic, doable and agile, rather than putting on your to-do list a case to upgrade your unit 'some day'.

When one person in the group shows up differently, they change how things have been done up until now in the group. And change by change, you lead your group towards a new way of interacting and thinking. One shift at a time, you can alter the group identity in your unit.

To drive change and shift mindsets across other levels, units and groups in the organization, you need to master the political chessboard.

The next section to elevate your environment delves into the dreamland of 'politics'.

Strategy 3: Master the political chessboard

To engage others in change, progress through thresholds in their careers or shape organizational culture, leaders need to navigate the mindsets of the people they interact with and the organizational frameworks.

As leaders strive to drive growth across different levels in the organization and build momentum, they can face various obstacles. These include processes or people that do not promote innovation or agility, differing views and standards, conflicting agendas, resistance to change or difficulty accessing and gaining visibility with senior leadership.

Leaders seek to navigate those by polishing their influencing skills to engage stakeholders and developing their brand to gain sponsors. What Sushant, and many leaders, refers to as 'doing politics'.

However, their efforts and the time and energy they invest in politics do not always translate into differential outputs that advance their visions and enable them to break through growth thresholds and gain momentum. When this happens, they risk being put off by engaging in these manoeuvres.

Politics can end up being a frustrating, complex or draining experience for leaders, that can emerge as games of power, authority and competition. They also perceive them as layers of status that are difficult to intervene in and get through or as a blockage to promoting agility, new ideas or their own growth.

Leaders' views and experiences about politics, as well as the tactics to navigate them, can result in low-impact and inefficient interactions that prevent them from engaging in conversations and political strategies that translate into advancement at scale and momentum.

To gain an edge in engaging and mobilizing others in change and promoting transformation, leaders need to rise above these dynamics and shift how they approach their political strategy and moves.

This section explores how to craft a powerful case for others to vote for and the four political moves to engage others in it.

Beyond hierarchy, status and power: transformation at the core of political moves

Sushant was in touch with customers' needs, market trends and evolution of technology. He could not help but see the gap between where he was now and where his division could be.

He envisioned developing and improving solutions that would give his company an edge over competitors. However, other members of his organization did not have the same disruptive appetite as him or would not engage in his ideas, frustrating his aspirations and eagerness to achieve them quickly.

He would explain his slow and low progress because of the culture, people resisting change and his avoidance to engage in 'politics'. Thinking this way was preventing him from re-evaluating his strategy to engage others and honing the skills needed to challenge stakeholders' mindset and drive the change he envisioned.

When leaders encounter governance and people obstacles progressing through growth thresholds, promoting new ideas or implementing cultural change, they may inadvertently focus too much on these challenges, risking disconnection from their overarching vision. However, it's exactly their vision that is the vehicle to resonate with others, ignite their enthusiasm and foster alignment or common ground for driving change and advancing the organization.

Leaving ideologies and ethics of political initiatives on the side, the core of a politician's mentality and intention is to gain people's vote for a vision they have.

This means that to engage others, you need to become a master politician by presenting them with a vision they understand, connect with and see the potential for their growth. Whether it's to challenge your product team, aim for a promotion, build partnerships or look for your next career move.

Your edge to influence others lies in your capacity to craft and present a competitive and powerful vision that is inspiring for them, not just yourself. And they will engage in the measure they can lever to achieve growth from such vision.

Think of it as if you were building a trampoline.

The more capable you are of building a trampoline where others see they can jump and thrive, the more they'll join in with you. As you build a higher platform, you operate under a bigger lever for you and others in your organization to jump higher.

Many leaders have not done the work of building a trampoline for more players to jump on, reducing their advantage to influence others. They have not considered or communicated the potential of a vision and what would give other players a differential edge if they got on board. As a result, what they bring to the table gravitates more towards their personal agendas, views or aspirations, making it much harder for them to gain buy-in from the stakeholders they want to engage.

You need to think of your agenda as your individual trampoline.

Your individual trampoline is not a platform persuasive enough for others to jump on because there is no space for them to do so, and it's not a lever big enough for them to jump higher. As a result, it becomes much harder for you to engage others – the reverse is the same where it will be harder for others to engage you on their individual trampolines. The only possible conversation ends up being: 'your trampoline or mine?' (your agenda versus mine).

Your efforts will be better applied to building a bigger trampoline and presenting it to others so that they can jump in and gain an edge from a bigger lever to reach higher.

This trampoline analogy illustrates what can happen in your organization and with your vision. Aiming to gain buy-in for your individual agenda when it represents such a small lever for others to grow will lead you to engage in low-impact and inefficient interactions at a one-to-one level such as: 'your interests versus mine', 'your disruption appetite versus mine' or 'your agility standards versus mine'.

Your efforts to persuade others to jump in will be better applied in crafting and communicating a case that factors in an upside potential for others. You need to build a common winning case.

When you've built a case that others can relate to and benefit from, you can interact with others within the frame of such vision. You raise the focus from a one-to-one level of individual agendas and different views, styles and even personalities to a case that promotes you, the other players and the bigger system.

Putting a winning case at the core of your political moves raises the level of the conversation from inefficient and low-impact one-to-one level interactions that focus on individual agendas to a new space of possibilities that results in more generative conversations to engage others and manoeuvre change.

To achieve this, you need to build a trampoline that would make them jump and campaign as a master politician, encouraging others to join in.

Four political moves anchored in your case to elevate your campaign

What would give you an edge in gaining traction and engagement within the system is understanding the person in front of you – understanding what would make them jump or why it has not happened yet.

Instead of focussing on your brand, laying the groundwork and being prepared, what would give you an edge is considering these two aspects:

- How does my vision look from the other side?
- How does the other person gain an edge by buying-in (by jumping in)?

There are four moves we'll explore to look at your political strategy through a new lens:

    i.   Understand the player and sketch their world.
   ii.   Map and stretch your edge.
  iii.   Stand on the big trampoline.
  iv.   Give them a hook: the power of small pilots.

First move: understand the player and sketch their world

To have someone jump on your trampoline, you need to understand what would make them jump. If you don't know this, you need to observe them and/or ask them.

This move requires you to understand the stand they take, their drivers, their barriers to growth and their environment. Considering the following questions will help you explore this:

1. What does company, team and individual success look like for this player?
2. What would this player like to have accomplished a year from now? Why?

3. What *three* barriers do they need to overcome to achieve this?
4. What would this player like to be known for?
5. How is this player connected? Who are their stakeholders, and what are these stakeholders holding them accountable to?
6. Who would this player like to influence inside and outside the organization? What would this give them that they don't already have?
7. What are the blind spots or limitations of this player's strategy?

Or the million-dollar question: *What does this person want to drive forward? (What's their trampoline?)*

You can consider this for an individual player, a coalition of players, a division or even a company when you're thinking about building external partnerships. In the questions above, change *player* for *coalition*, *group* or *company* as needed.

These questions don't require you to have more or less status than someone; you need to observe them with a strategic lens. For this, you need to create the space to assess this person from a distance and their system to sketch their world.

Your key to success is understanding not only the person but also their bigger system. Factoring in their team's and stakeholders' success allows you to present to them a bigger lever for their advancement.

Second move: map and stretch your edge

In the same way you sketch the other player's system beyond just themselves, you need to sketch your system beyond your own persona to stretch the edge you bring to the synergy or coalition.

You first need to map your edge before you put it at the service of the other player.

Map your edge

To map your edge, you need to map your case and your resources:

- *Mapping your case* involves shaping and strengthening your business case that you want the other player to bet on. This requires you to explore and connect with your stand to advance your industry, wow customers and/or address inefficiencies in your organization. Or similarly, you can reconnect to the vision you drew in the 'Elevate your vision' pillar.
- *Mapping your resources* involves unpacking what you bring to the table to deliver on that case to support the other player's case. For this, connect with your expertise and experience and factor in your system, exploring your team, connections and stakeholders.

Stretch your edge

To stretch your edge, you need to make it valuable to the other player in the context of the successes they want to achieve, barriers they need to overcome and positioning they want to gain. This requires you to explore how your edge supports the other player to tackle the aspirations and challenges you drew from the previous move (understand the player and sketch their world) in the short, medium and long term.

The table below can help you with this. The idea is that you answer the question on the left for each one of the insights you gained from the previous move that appear in the right column.

For example: How can my leadership case, expertise, team and connections contribute to [*this person's company, team and individual success*] in the short, medium or long term?

Stretch your edge	
MY EDGE	**THE OTHER PLAYER'S**
	Company, team and individual success
How can my leadership	1-year accomplishments
case, expertise, team and	Barriers to overcome
connections contribute to	Credibility/positioning
[*this insight*] in the short,	Stakeholders' requests
medium or long term?	Influence strategy
	Blind spots

With a wider and more strategic understanding of the player and what you bring, you have gained a new edge and positioned yourself on a wider platform from where to have the conversation. You've built a bigger trampoline; a common case involves a new space of possibilities for you, them and your systems.

This bigger trampoline or common case is the frame of your conversation with other players.

Third move: stand on the big trampoline (aka: don't jump off!)

When you stand on the trampoline and speak from this place, you have raised the focus from one-to-one agendas to a new space of possibilities you want to engage others in. To gain an influential advantage in the conversation, you need to speak from this trampoline.

To stand on the trampoline, you need to follow this counterintuitive strategy: don't jump off it.

It seems pretty obvious, but it is not.

You're on the trampoline when you focus on the common case and the synergy with the other player, and you jump off it when you shift the focus to individual agendas, lowering the level of the conversation. Unfortunately, jumping off it can happen subconsciously, rapidly and often. The reason for this is your identity, which can trigger you to jump off it when situations don't evolve as you would have hoped for.

Like everyone, you have your own views, ideas, standards, aspirations and preferences that might differ from others. When you share yours and there is a mismatch between what you envision and where the other person or group stands, your identity interprets this situation. The problem for your political strategy arises when these interpretations lead you to move away from the space of synergies and possibilities.

Sometimes these interpretations can emerge as stories evaluating the other person, your efforts or the culture such as: 'I'm handholding for change.' 'She has a big ego.' 'My company does not embrace disruptors.' 'He is a narcist.' 'It's a competitive environment.' 'There is internal competition.'

While you might experience being held back by others or the culture to some degree, this is just an interpretation your identity is making that can keep you in a box from next-level results. If you're not aware of how your identity functions and don't upgrade it to shift your focus and explore new resourceful behaviours, then, consciously or subconsciously, you solely fixate on this interpretation and you can jump off the trampoline. As a result, you step out of the winning case and the land of possibilities and synergies, thereby losing your edge to influence others.

When you jump off the trampoline because you are triggered by your identity, you have a smaller lever from where to lead the conversation and risk engaging in low-impact interactions that block advancement and generate frustration.

To avoid jumping off the trampoline, you need to become aware of when, why and by whom your identity is triggered. By acknowledging and bringing these narratives to the surface, you can be aware of them and challenge them to refine your political strategy.

For example, Sushant's identity was triggered when peers would challenge the need for a new solution. This led him to engage in stories about people or culture not promoting change and innovation and that others did not align to the degree of transformation or speed he envisioned. These stories made him jump off the trampoline and prevented him from exploring what he needed to say and how to elevate his political strategy and make others jump in.

In any company, there are going to be competing agendas, diverse personalities and ways of thinking, and different perspectives on the pace for change that is required. What would give you an edge is seeing beyond the one-to-one discrepancies and obstacles and engaging with people from a place of possibilities that they're not seeing, but you do.

To keep your focus on the trampoline and engage in more generative conversations, you can consider questions such as:

1. What's the missing opportunity for this person and the company if they don't jump in? A month from now, a quarter from now, a year from now?
2. How is this person losing time, profit, impact and engagement for not being on board?
3. What do you see and know from your position that they don't that would advance them and your organization?
4. How do they measure success and how do they speak about it so you can factor it into your conversations?

From the trampoline, you can always offer them a hook to jump in.

Fourth move: give them a hook: the power of small pilots

Don't lead only with your words; provide players with tangible evidence and results that act as a hook.

The idea of this move is that you share test results from a small pilot of a new initiative you've started to work on, implement or research, and present your findings and the next steps. You can also share with them a survey, an analysis of competitors' practices and reports on market trends sourced from the sales department.

A tangible hook can engage others in a vision or idea that they still perceive as abstract, not needed, difficult to implement or not impactful by shifting their focus to their tangible potential or a clear path to action. You can gain an edge in your political strategy when you show people who resist change and naysayers how it can be done and what your vision or idea looks like because you've started to explore it and implement it.

This move can help you optimize your efforts and elevate your political strategy by engaging others in something that already works.

To leverage it, think about the gap in mindset and perspective between where you're at and where the person is that you want to engage. Start by exploring the need you see for change, the potential you see in your idea and how you measure progress, impact and growth, that the other person or people in the room don't see. Then bridge that gap with evidence.

Let the evidence and results challenge their view, resistances or metrics. Then have a conversation from a different place with the new insights they've gained.

~

These four political moves will help you manoeuvre the organizational system and engage external stakeholders.

Move by move, person by person, you can master the political chessboard and bring others to new places. As you challenge organizational structures and mindsets, you are stretching out the company's edges.

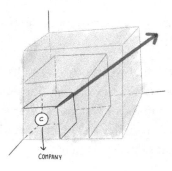

COMPANY

Change at scale won't happen overnight, but the moves you can make to engage players in the system do. To succeed in these political moves, you need to go into the fishbowl to reflect on and plan your manoeuvres. Use the next activity to help you do this.

Become a master politician with four political moves

Identify the one key player you would like to bring on board that would twice increase your growth and momentum in the month ahead. Consider the following questions:

1. **The player**: what's holding back this person and their system from the next level of growth, success and influence?

2. **Your edge**: what's the edge you bring to their case? How can you – your case, expertise, team and connections – make this person and their system more successful in the short, medium and long term?

3. **Stand on the trampoline**:

   - What triggers you to jump off the trampoline when engaging with this person? Consider *what* they say or *how* they say it.

   - What is the missing opportunity in time and/or profit, if they're not on board? A month from now, a year from now?

4. **Hook**: which results or evidence does this person need to see to be on board?

Fundamentals

- Environment sets performance. It acts as a **propulsor** to generate momentum and as a **catapult** to reach higher levels.

- You can be a catalyst or a victim of it. To upgrade it you need to master its **paradox** by assessing the system complexity with a helicopter view and harnessing the power of micro-interactions and manoeuvres.

- There are three environmental strategies:

  1. **Foster a team of A-players**
     - Focus on the individuals' transformation in your one-to-one interactions. Go beyond project status and technicalities and draw them out with questions.
     - To become a coach, you need *a three-pillar model* and an *identity* to build a case for their development and show up intentionally in conversations.

  2. **Create units of excellence**
     - Catalyse a bottom-up change by elevating the conditions and interactions in the groups you can influence.
     - Upgrade your group identity: identify group *dialogues and dynamics (D^2)* that block advancement and transformation to intervene in them one shift at a time.

3. **Master the political chessboard**
   - Move beyond low-impact and inefficient interactions at a one-to-one level and put your case for transformation at the core of your political strategy.
   - Build a winning case for others to jump in with *four political moves*:
     i. Understand the player and sketch their world.
     ii. Map and stretch your edge.
     iii. Stand on the trampoline by keeping an eye on your identity and focussing on possibilities.
     iv. Give them a hook leveraging the power of small pilots.

Into the fishbowl: catalyse your environment in the next month

 Identify specific people and situations to upgrade your environment in the month ahead. Consider the activities shared for each strategy.

1. Who is **one team member** I would like to coach, in the month ahead? *(Activity: become a coach; assess your team members to build a case for their development.)*

2. Which **meeting** do I want to upgrade with my team or peer group in the month ahead? *(Activity: assess and elevate your group identity.)*

3. Which **key player** would I like to bring on board in the month ahead? *(Activity: become a master politician with four political moves.)*

Part III
The two
insatiable
meta-abilities

The previous chapters explored the three-pillar elevation model. To create next-level results, you need to:

- take a stand and craft a pioneer vision.
- upgrade your identity to lead such vision to the highest standards.
- hone the conditions in your environment to inject momentum, sustain your growth and look up to new growth thresholds.

The model is designed to bring leaders to new spaces from where to keep growing. However, for leaders to be able to tackle the three pillars repeatedly and fuel continuous growth, the model needs a transversal factor across the pillars – the insatiable meta-abilities: non-linear time management and presence.

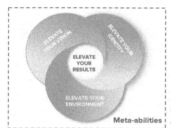

Non-linear time management
Meta-abilities *Presence*

These two meta-abilities govern the model.

Bringing back the mountain analogy, you can think of them as a master programme to support transformation across each pillar and unlock new growth thresholds ongoingly.

We delve into them in this third and last part of the book.

Chapter 6

Meta-abilities: tools for limitless growth

This chapter sheds light on the two insatiable meta-abilities: non-linear time management and presence.

By the end of this chapter, you will:

- discover their catalytic power to fuel ongoing transformation and achieve next-level results.
- explore three alternative strategies to create time.
- learn how to cultivate and master presence across its three dimensions.

The hallmark of insatiability: an ongoing growth journey

'Excellence is never an accident. It is always the result of high intention, sincere effort, and intelligent execution; it represents the wise choice of many alternatives – choice, not chance, determines your destiny.'

Aristotle

To Lauren

How to make an outstanding leader catalyse even more impact? That's what I have in mind when I think about Lauren.

> I first came across her profile in the Forbes 30 Under 30 list, which selects 30 outstanding profiles less than 30 years old based on their revenue, social impact and potential in their industries. A hub for insatiable leaders.

> After a decade in investment banking, Lauren carved her own path as an inclusion and diversity leader. She became a pioneer in Equity, Diversity and Inclusion (ED&I) in every company she had worked for, shaping and scaling diversity strategies to impact talent, clients and communities globally.

> Our coaching engagement evolved around her first role at C-Level as Chief ED&I Officer in a food and beverage company to set the global ED&I strategy for the first time in the organization.

> She needed to operate at a new level of leadership to shape a vision to leave a legacy of diversity in her organization, build and grow a global team of contributors across borders and engage her ecosystem in her vision of change – from workers in the factories to clients to the board. She basically needed to tackle the three pillars of the model.

By the end of our engagement, she asked me a set of questions to review her growth and help her to keep growing in the future. There is one that hit me and holds the clue for this chapter.

"How could I have gotten more from the coaching programme?" she asked.

As I was hit by her insatiable essence in action, I turned that question back to her; a typical move we coaches have to answer people with questions.

She gave herself one key answer: "With more time."

I gave her the other: "With more presence."

Time and presence: enablers and catalysts of growth

A leader's development depends on the quality of insights they generate to access new growth thresholds and their commitment to allocate space for this process. For this they need both time and presence – an inner state of calm, awareness and resourcefulness essential to generate powerful insights.

This is easier said than done.

Leaders' calendars are often packed, leaving little space to strategically think about their business, their leadership and their environment. Moreover, as they seek to create time, the time management techniques they use don't always enable them to create more hours, reorganize their calendars and create space for self-reflection.

Equally, these busy schedules and hectic rhythms contribute to a constant buzz of activity in their minds, preventing them from being present. This hinders their awareness and resourcefulness in critical situations, limiting their capacity to consider new perspectives to fuel transformation and act on them in the moment.

To solve this, they need to create time with alternative time management techniques that gives them the hours they seek to develop and cultivate presence. To progress across the three pillars, they need to master the two meta-abilities: non-linear time management and presence.

The focus of the next two sections is to explain each meta-ability and the strategies to develop them.

Meta-ability 1: Non-linear time management

Before delving into what non-linear time management is, it's essential to first understand the concept of linear time management and its limitations in enabling leaders to create time as they chart new growth thresholds.

Linear time management results in an unending procession of tasks that extends indefinitely into the future, consistently packing leaders' calendars with an ever-growing workload.

Through this perspective, leaders seek to master their time with methods and strategies such as allocating time for deep work; identifying what to do, decide, delegate or delete; batching similar tasks; and 'eating frogs' first thing in the morning.[1]

While these techniques are essential to amplify focus, elevate productivity and progress with the workflow of tasks, they don't always enable leaders to rise up from the never-ending linearity of tasks into a space for innovation and fresh thinking to create next-level results and pursue new growth opportunities.

Non-linear time management involves introducing a substantial change in that linearity of never-ending tasks so that you can upgrade your calendar to the new space in which you're leading your vision.

Incremental adjustments in your calendar and optimizing your minutes and tasks won't enable you to upgrade your calendar so that it supports your vision. You need to make substantial, non-linear changes.

Introducing a factor of non-linearity in your vision as you stretch your aspirations and craft a pioneer vision requires that your calendar supports that non-linearity.

In this section, we will explore the basis of non-linear time management and three non-linear strategies to upgrade your calendar to your stretched vision and support your aspirations.

Managing your time is not a task game, but an identity one

'Manage perceptions, not circumstances.'

Steve Chandler

In his book *Time Warrior*, Steve Chandler emphasizes how linear time management does not work because it does not account for perceptions, only circumstances.

Managing circumstances involves evaluating your events and tasks in your calendar, considering what they require from you, determining who in your team can do them, estimating how much time they'll take and deciding when to do them – now, next week, postpone, or never. The focus is on assessing and dissecting the task and events.

Managing your perceptions involves understanding how you relate to and interpret those circumstances, tasks and everything around them. The focus is on you first. This requires you to intervene at the identity level.

Your identity plays a significant role in your time management choices and habits. These are influenced by your self-conception, your interpretation of circumstances and other's responses, as well as your perception of others' capabilities. To get to the core of what's behind inefficient ways of managing your calendar, you need to comprehend the system of attachment and aversions that holds your identity in place.

As discussed earlier in this book, our identity operates under a system of attachments and aversions at a very subtle level. Attachment towards what we want or perceive as positive or familiar, such as longing for approval, sense of competence or being considered as a capable leader. Aversion towards what we don't want, dislike or is unfamiliar, such as fear to say no or experiencing guilt.

Understanding how your identity operates is critical because it influences your time choices. Engaging with these inner drivers can lead to inefficient time choices and stories to justify them. These choices risk being at the service of your identity and what you subconsciously seek to reinforce or avoid, but not always at the service of your vision and what's required from you as a leader.

These inefficient 'identity time choices' can result in overcommitment, perfectionism or subconsciously using time to gain approval or please others. They can also make leaders believe that they complete tasks more impactfully or efficiently than others or that they are indispensable in some situations, thereby preventing them from delegating or changing anything in their calendars.

Your identify can lead you to engage in patterns, stories and habits that perpetuate inefficient time choices about how you organize your calendar, sometimes without you realizing. When this happens, you end up trapped in a box.

To break out of it and make quantum leaps in creating time, you need to surface, challenge and upgrade your identity.

The reason why some time management tools can be inefficient is because they don't intervene at the identity level and don't account for perceptions. My experience is that many leaders attribute the problem with time to their circumstances, the workload, the need for more hours or the need for new time management techniques to improve their efficiency. However, they have not stopped to challenge how their identities and subconscious inner drivers are responsible and perpetuate their hectic calendars and lack of time.

Without engaging in this introspection and intervening at the identity level to understand the drivers that influence your time choices, you risk being a victim of circumstances, running behind the aspirations you want to pursue. You'll be trapped in a box by your identity and your habits, regardless of how efficiently you optimize your minutes and how much you improve your productivity.

To break out of this trap, you need to audit, understand and challenge how your identity prevents you from making new time choices that support the vision you're leading and rising above the never-ending linearity of tasks.

Three strategies to create time that are not about productivity

These are three recurrent identity traps I see leaders fall into that prevent them from creating time:

- They buy into the story that there is no time and what they need is more hours.
- They're unaware that their calendar choices are influenced by emotional drivers such as guilt or seeking to prove or please.
- They think they don't need space to think strategically.

The following strategies will help you to audit your calendar to overcome these pitfalls:

i.   Time deprivation.
ii. Emotional (time) management.
iii. Bend time with strategic thinking time.

As you consider the exercises that I'll suggest, I invite you to print your calendar for the last three weeks. It will be eye-opening as you audit it with the first two strategies, as Lauren did.

Strategy 1: Time deprivation

"I don't have time," Lauren said, as we reviewed the adjustments she would need to introduce in her calendar.

She did not only say it, but she showed me her calendar, as many leaders do, to back up the case that there is no time.

"Look," she continued, "there is literally no space."

Her calendar was indeed packed, and there was clearly not much space. But she was trapped by inefficient patterns that would not enable her to rise above this.

Lauren was wired to take on new meetings as circumstances changed or responsibilities increased, stretching herself to deliver on them and wishing she had more time or was more efficient and productive at dealing with everything in her calendar. She was trapped by her identity, defaulting to habits and perceptions about herself and the capacity to do everything that prevented her from creating the space she needed.

To rise above this, she needed to shift her focus and challenge her thinking. Instead of considering the scenario where she would have more time, the clue was to put her in an opposite scenario in which she was deprived of it.

It involved considering a hypothetical scenario in which she had four hours less of time a week. This challenge required her to stretch her thinking to find alternatives not to optimize her minutes, but to introduce drastic changes in her calendar. By removing from the equation what she thought she needed, which was more hours or stretching herself to deliver on everything, she was forced to look at her calendar through a new lens.

As you experiment with this strategy of being deprived of time, imagine yourself in a situation where you have had four hours less each week for the past three weeks. These are four hours that you would need to gain back as they're allocated now.

Simply wondering what would change if you had four hours less a week is not a question to merely contemplate. When leaders radically consider and answer it, they move from the mindset of 'nothing in my calendar can go' to identifying activities and meetings that they can delegate, reassign and re-structure in duration, purpose or time. They're stretched in their thinking and unlock a new space of possibilities.

But why four hours when you are already experiencing time starvation?

The more you stretch that number of hours you seek to deprive yourself of, the more you'll be stretched in your thinking to consider new possibilities you did not see before. If you only experimented with 30 minutes of time deprivation, the stretch in your thinking would be minimal.

The objective of this strategy is beyond actually creating a few minutes. It's rather about stretching your thinking as if you had four hours less and considering more drastic possibilities to reorganize your calendar.

As Mark Manson observes: 'We are defined by what we choose to reject.'

Choosing might not always be obvious but failing to 'choose to reject something' leaves you at the mercy of circumstances. To avoid drifting you need to step back and assess your choices anchored in your stand, your vision and case.

Consider the questions below in this activity for this strategy. Don't only read them, give them an answer, and you'll start looking at your calendar differently to create time.

Create time with time deprivation

Looking at your *printed* calendar over the last three weeks, consider the following questions:

1. **Stretch**: If you had four working hours less each week, what would go or what would change in your calendar?

    Consider for example:

    - If you needed to change the *duration of three* meetings, which ones would they be and why?
    - If you needed to adapt the *frequency of three* meetings, which ones would they be and why?
    - Looking at your three weeks, what are the tasks, meetings and appointments that can *only be done*

> *by you* and where your presence is indispensable
> – i.e. the meetings that no one in your team could
> take on, even if coached?
>
> 2. **Adjust**: Based on the insights above, what are the
>   *three* adjustments you can make in your calendar to
>   reorganize your team members in the week ahead?

Wanting more hours is not the only trap that prevented Lauren and other leaders from upgrading their calendars. Guided by their own wiring, they can use time as a vehicle to prove, please or validate their status, and they don't introduce substantial changes in their calendars for fear of rejection, guilt or how they might be perceived.

Consciously or subconsciously, at some level, they lead their calendars with their emotional drivers at the core of their identity that caps transformation.

Strategy 2: Emotional (time) management

To master non-linear time management, you need to manage your perceptions, and this involves factoring in the personal significance and interpretation you attach to circumstances and changes in your calendar.

What would give you an edge in this strategy is intervening at the core of your identity's attachment and aversions and the emotions they can trigger.

Subconsciously, we are naturally drawn towards experiences we desire, such as seeking approval, recognition, and feelings of competency and legitimacy. Conversely, we tend to avoid situations that evoke, for example, fear, resistance, confrontations with norms or feelings of guilt.

These emotional drivers can lead to inefficient time choices in your calendar such as:

- keeping commitments and meetings in your calendar for fear of saying no or questioning in the group the relevance, duration or structure of such meetings.
- investing time and energy in tasks and meetings as a vehicle for gaining approval, pleasing, proving or validating your competence or status.
- keeping tasks for resistance or fear to lose control or supervision over some projects or clients, preventing you from coaching your team members on them.
- dedicating time to tasks you do well or know how to manage to appear as if you have been productive or busy, instead of focussing on tasks that will support leading in a new space. The latter are tasks that are often perceived as difficult, question your competence or require you to operate in the domain of risk or potential rejection, generating aversion at the identity level.

Leaders can be trapped in their calendars by the subconscious drivers of their of identities. As a result, they make time choices based on how they want to be perceived by others and their fears or desires, rather than by choices that support the vision they lead.

To get out of this trap, you need to surface those inefficient time choices. You need to challenge what's behind the time choices based on how you interact with people and your own emotions and elicit how your system of attachments and aversions leads to inefficient ways of allocating time.

Create time with emotional (time) management

Looking at your *printed* calendar over the last three weeks, consider the following questions:

1. What are the top *three* activities/meetings/appointments/ tasks you use to fill time to feel as though you've been *productive or busy*?
2. If you did not feel *guilty*, what are the top *three* activities you would remove or adapt from your calendar?
3. What are the *three* top activities you're doing to *prove* something to others or yourself? E.g. to validate your legitimacy, gain recognition, etc.
4. What are the *three* top activities you're doing to *please*?
5. What are the main *three* tasks or meetings that you believe *your team cannot handle* without your supervision?
6. Based on the insights above, consider:

    - What are the *three adjustments* you can make in your calendar and reorganize your team members for the week ahead?

These two strategies will help you gain awareness about inefficient default habits and start considering new possibilities to introduce substantial changes in your calendar and commitments.

But to create time with them you need *time* to reflect on your calendar.

What a scam.

What will enable you to create time is, ironically, creating strategic thinking space. This strategic thinking space is critical not only to strategize about your calendar but also to go into the fishbowl and gain new insights to lead your business, yourself and your environment more efficiently.

Strategy 3: Bend time with strategic thinking time

Achieving outstanding results quickly and efficiently requires optimizing your choices and strategies.

Being fully immersed in her day-to-day activities, in her ocean, prevented Lauren from considering other manoeuvres to advance her business, herself and others in her system. By creating distance and going into the fishbowl, she could gain perspective and insights to consider more impactful, efficient and strategic possibilities to show up in her day-to-day situations, enabling her to inject velocity in elevating her results at an individual, group and company level.

Nevertheless, many leaders postpone, disregard or avoid going into the fishbowl. Influenced by their identities, they believe that they can make strides in their growth and enhance their efficiency without creating time and space to strategically think about their business, their leadership and their environment.

Each leader has their own story, and I'm sure you have yours.

The best way to determine whether creating strategic thinking space and going into the fishbowl makes a difference in your advancement is by experiencing it first-hand. At the end of this chapter, you'll find an 'into the fishbowl challenge' to create 30 minutes for strategic thinking time each week for two months (totalling four hours in two months), along with a suggested roadmap for each week with the 'into the fishbowl activities' and strategies explored in this book. You can also access it via this link: https://insatiable-leaders.com/book-bonus

After engaging with this experiment, you can evaluate based on your own experience whether creating strategic thinking space can inject velocity into your journey and elevate your results.

If you're pondering whether to try this experiment, I invite you to challenge your identity that makes you believe that you can make strides in your growth without creating strategic thinking space.

> ### Create time by challenging your time identity around strategic thinking time
>
> The question to consider is:
>
> * What's behind the illusion that you can make leaps in your growth and efficiency without allocating 30 minutes of strategic thinking time this week?

These three strategies are designed to help you create time, reorganize your calendar and make new leadership choices that translate into increased efficiency. However, these yields can be significantly hindered by the mental activity that prevents you from fully maximizing your time and focus to produce impactful outputs in the present moment.

How much time do you lose for not being present?

Meta-ability 2: Presence

One connotation of presence is the gravitas to take command of a room, inspire confidence in an audience and impress or influence others.

That's a game to master outside yourself. The presence we will explore in this section is a game that happens inside yourself.

Presence is an inner state of inclusive and immediate awareness of your business, yourself and the system you operate in that reveals new possibilities and choices to contribute to the most extensive possible context.[2]

Presence has three dimensions you need to differentiate:

* The qualities of this inner state and what's required from you to *access* it.
* The *experience or revelation* of this state – a larger context of possibilities and connectedness.
* The *implications* of this state.

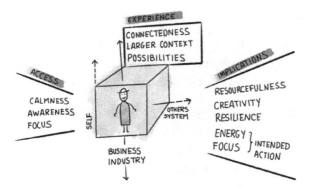

By deepening your awareness, calmness and focus, presence enables you to gain a new understanding and clarity of how everything is connected throughout you simultaneously – how you connect to your business, yourself, your system and others – revealing a larger context and new insights that you did not see before.

With a renewed sense of possibilities and interconnections as implications of this state, leaders see new choices to behave and interact in more creative and resourceful ways within their context, with themselves and their environment to support their commitment and visions.

The focus of this section is to delve into the importance of presence in your day-to-day transformation and how to cultivate it.

Presence: an immediate doorway for transformation that many leaders miss

You might have experienced presence through the book answering the questions you've found through the chapters. They are intended to increase your awareness about your situation, unlock new possibilities for transformation and foster a sense of resourcefulness to behave in different ways. That's the experience and power of presence.

While it's important to take a step back to strategically reflect about a situation, either with hindsight or for preparation, the quality of presence is that it's immediate; it happens in the moment.

The present is where the biggest possibilities for growth lie.

The present is where the market is at any moment, revealing new opportunities and problems that you can address to shape new strategies to gain an edge as a company and as an individual.

The present is when you default into a habit to respond to a situation that leads you to inefficient results, and that moment of choice where you realize that you can explore more creative and resourceful ways to behave to support your aspirations.

The present is when you observe how agendas conflict in a meeting, blocking transformation or reinforcing the status quo, and the realization that you can intervene in the interaction and create alignment and engagement amongst your peers to support a vision that advances the system.

Being present catalyses your transformation and results for each one of the pillars in the moment.

It takes one second to be present if you shift and channel your focus and are aware of yourself within the bigger context – market, stakeholders, clients – and find connections between these elements that reveal new possibilities.

The bigger your capacity to be aware of how you connect with what's happening in your context to access it and influence it, the bigger transformation you'll spark, without postponing it for later or preparing for it.

However, leaders risk rushing through the present or not being fully immersed in it, which prevents them from realizing how everything connects through them and responding in more resourceful and creative ways that support the results they want to create at every moment of their journey.

When Lauren was not in a state of calm and awareness in her day-to-day activities and was trapped in her busyness, hectic schedule and noise in her mind, she was missing the potential of transformation that the present moment offered her.

The sessions were a space for strategic thinking time and presence; however, this was only for an hour. Her potential to unlock higher levels of growth depended on extending this state of presence and its qualities of calm, sharpened focus and awareness throughout her day to reveal new possibilities for transformation.

To maximize the potential for the transformation she could drive in every moment, she needed to increase her capacity to be in the present. And for this, she needed to practise, develop and master presence.

Cultivate presence across its three dimensions

To cultivate presence, you need to bring your attention to the three dimensions explored earlier; accessing this state by developing its qualities, expanding the revelations of this state, and harnessing the implications of it.

These are three strategies to help you foster your growth in each dimension:

   i.   Build a habit of developing the qualities to access presence.
   ii. Expand connectedness and possibilities.
   iii. Identify opportunities for growth to show up resourcefully.

Build a habit of developing the qualities to access presence

Dropping into presence requires accessing a state of calmness, awareness and focus. By shifting your state and quieting your mind, you can create space for powerful insights.

To reinforce this state, you need to build a habit about it to cultivate these qualities. In this link (https://www.insatiable-leaders.com/book-bonus) you'll find a 5-minute body scan and breathing exercise for this purpose. You can do it at the start of your day, before an important meeting or even before starting your *30 minutes of strategic thinking space* to maximize the power of your insights.

You can use this exercise or whichever other form you choose to shift your state and sharpen your awareness about how you relate with your market, clients, yourself and others. You might choose to take three deep breaths or meditate for 10 minutes, but know that to develop presence, you need time to reinforce accessing this state and developing its qualities. And you need to build a habit to develop those.

There is no shortcut to cultivate this habit. Without calm, sharpened focus and awareness, the quality of your insights diminishes and with it the potential to maximize the power of transformation offered by the present moment.

Expand connectedness and possibilities

Once you access this state, you can reveal new information in your context through your own experience and observation.

The transformational questions in this book are designed for this purpose. These powerful questions are the doorway to generate elevated insights because they turn the focus inwards so that you look to your business, the market, yourself, your system and others through a new lens to see new possibilities and interconnections. These are the questions that will enable you to generate new insights and foster growth in your *30 minutes of strategic thinking space.*

The power of these questions is everlasting. If you ask yourself the same question every week, every month or every quarter, your insights will be different each time. While the questions are the same, you will always generate new possibilities for transformation and advancement in your system.

As you use these questions recurrently with hindsight or for preparation in your fishbowl, you strengthen your capacity to expand your sense of connectedness and deepen your awareness about your context in your day-to-day activities – in the moment.

Identify opportunities for growth to show up resourcefully

With a renewed sense of possibilities, you will see new choices and opportunities to show up and behave in more resourceful, creative and resilient ways.

To cultivate this dimension of presence, you need to translate the insights you have generated into clear opportunities for action, with a defined timeframe to enhance your accountability and support your transformation.

You need to identify and declare the growth opportunities in the week or month ahead to lead your business, yourself or others differently by applying those insights. To enhance your transformation, you need to be specific about which situation, when and with whom to prompt you to action. The questions and strategies in the chapters have been crafted to foster your growth in this dimension of presence, encouraging you to channel your insights into clear steps for action.

This might seem like an obvious step, but it's not. Insights and actions take place in two different dimensions – your mind and the world where results happen. Therefore, it's crucial not to leave insights as mere ideas in your head; instead, translate them into clear opportunities for action that prompt you to lean in differently.

As you reinforce your awareness about a situation in which you want to show up differently, you increase and reinforce your capacity to respond in creative ways as similar situations or interactions repeat in your day-to-day activities. With practice, you can respond in more resourceful and generative ways in the moment. But practising is key.

A path towards mastery: continually leaning in intentionally in the moment

Like any ability, it's something that you master as you practise.

In the beginning, you might only gain awareness about possibilities and new choices to show up differently with perspective, looking at a situation with hindsight or to prepare for it in the future. This is what you might have experienced through the book, or what you'll do as you create strategic thinking time to go into the fishbowl.

That's part of the journey, and it's critical to nurture the practice of presence. However, the more you practise the three steps – developing the qualities of presence, expanding connectedness and possibilities, and identifying new opportunities to show up resourcefully – the less you will need to think about being present and review what has happened in the past or prepare to bring intentionality to the future.

As you cultivate presence, you increase your awareness, enabling you to perceive and relate more to the elements in the moment. This equips you to respond in resourceful and creative ways more frequently and lead new possibilities to fuel transformation in the moment.

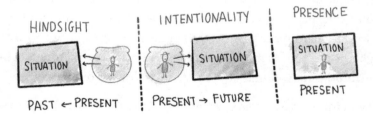

Developing presence enhances your readiness to lead in an ever-changing world, enabling you to identify opportunities for gaining an advantage and intervene in them. The higher your degree of presence, the higher your capacity for transformation in every moment along your journey.

Presence is an art. Master your presence, and you will master your leadership by catalysing intentional growth at every stage of your journey.

Fundamentals

- To progress across the three pillars, you need to master the two meta-abilities: non-linear time management and presence. These act as enablers to promote ongoing transformation and growth in your journey.

- **Non-linear time management** involves introducing drastic changes in your calendar to upgrade it to the non-linearity of your vision. It requires you to manage *perceptions* rather than circumstances and for this you need to intervene at the identity level.

- There are *three strategies* to break out of your box that perpetuates your inefficient time choices:

  i.   Time deprivation

  ii. Emotional (time) management

  iii. Create strategic thinking space to bend time

- **Presence** is an *inner state* of inclusive and immediate awareness, connectedness and resourcefulness in the space of transformation you lead.

- To master presence in the moment, you need to practice the *three strategies to cultivate the three dimensions* of presence:

  i   Build a habit to develop the qualities to access presence.

  ii   Expand connectedness and possibilities with transformational questions.

  iii Identify opportunities for growth to show up more resourcefully and creatively.

Into the fishbowl: into your fishbowl challenge

 If you were to take something from this book, commit to dedicating 30 minutes to strategic thinking over the next eight weeks, totalling four hours over the next two months.

Consider the roadmap below to reflect on critical topics to fuel transformation each week. For each week, revisit 'Into the fishbowl' dynamics and strategies shared throughout the book as indicated.

You can download the dynamics to complete each week from the following link: https://www.insatiable-leaders.com/book-bonus

Week	Focus
1	Create time using Strategy 1: Time depravation
2	Elevate your vision: draw a vision that provides you with a competitive advantage
3	Elevate your identity: bring intentionality to your journey. Explore your developmental edges in critical situations
4	Foster a team of A-players: Assess [person 1] in your team to build a case for their development and coach them
5	Create time using Strategy 2: Emotional (time) management
6	Create a high-performing *team*: assess and upgrade your team interactions
7	Create a high-performing *peer group*: assess and upgrade your peer group interactions
8	Master the political chessboard: become a master politician and plan your next political move

Choose after these eight weeks if strategic thinking time is something worth adding to your calendar or not.

Epilogue

One last dance: harness your insatiability

'People who are insatiable enough to question the limits are the ones who surpass them.'

Susana Martínez Denia

As I reflect back on the conversations I've had with leaders, what I've read and my own journey, I cannot but keep coming back to this idea: that insatiable leaders are wired to question and surpass the limits.

The leaders with this essence are a force to break through obstacles, challenging themselves in constant pursuit of the next aspiration, goal, challenge or space to explore. And they continually redefine and break through the limits imposed upon them.

While 'insatiable' implies an inability to be satisfied, which often carries a negative connotation, I believe the most crucial aspect of this word lies not in whether the satisfaction has been attained or not, but rather in the journey of transformation and contribution that leaders with this essence embark on in their pursuit.

The six traits at the core of this essence equip leaders who embrace them to bring themselves and others to new spaces, advance their organizations, make an impact in their industries and relentlessly deliver on those visions.

However, these traits act like a double-edged sword and can lead you to inefficiencies, frustration and exhaustion, limiting your advancement and growth journey.

Insatiability is a roller coaster. It's a dance between a world of possibilities, opportunities, impact and expansion; and a world of doubt, resistance, questioning, ineffectiveness and sometimes loneliness.

It's precisely in this dynamic tension between these two worlds that you can choose how you want to lead, what you want to lead and your growth experience in that journey.

To master this dance, you must master your traits by understanding them and channelling them to your advantage.

Insatiability is a dance that is always going on, at every stage of your growth journey. As it prompts you to break through limits and explore new spaces, it can also hold you back from thriving in them if you don't channel it.

To rise beyond this trap, the three-pillar model and the meta-abilities are your allies and partners in this dance to reach intentionally new growth thresholds continually.

You might have concluded that the approach to development that I present in this book does not lead to satisfaction, completion or a fulfilled state. That's an impossible solution for insatiability. Rather, it harnesses this essence to make that ongoing growth journey impactful and inspiring for you and others around you.

Insatiable means, indeed, impossible to satisfy. It implies a craving or a drive that persists despite efforts to fulfil it.

But why fulfil it? Or correct it? It's the engine for advancement and progression.

Rather than viewing this as a flaw to be suppressed or tamed, I call on leaders to nurture it and harness it to fuel progression and advancement in their organizations and growth journeys.

And I call you to do the same with yours.

Discover what you're hungry for in every step of your journey. And use it as a driving force to take a stand, propel yourself into the future, overcome barriers and inspire those around you to do the same.

My hope is that this book will have given you new insights, strategies and one or two questions to harness this essence and master your dance. If, at some moment, you play off-beat and need inspiration, you might find it at www.insatiable-leaders.com.

Thank you for sharing the journey through these pages with me.

Be insatiable,

Susana

Appendix A

Web-based resources

The following resources are available through the Insatiable Leaders website:

https://www.insatiable-leaders.com/book-bonus

1. Breathing exercise and body scan audio to cultivate your presence and reset your inner state.
2. Templates for the 'Into the fishbowl challenge' to create 30 minutes of strategic thinking space for eight weeks.
3. Downloadable summary featuring key sketches from the book.

Appendix B

Further reading

1. Gay Hendricks. *The Big Leap: Conquer Your Hidden Fear and Take Life to the Next Level.* 2010. This book will help you to identify and transcend your upper limit.

2. Doug Silsbee. *Presence-Based Leadership: Complexity Practices for Clarity, Resilience and Results that Matter.* 2018. A comprehensive book to master your presence to lead in complexity and challenge.

3. Mark Goulston. *Just Listen: Discover the Secret to Getting Through to Absolutely Anyone.* 2018. The subtitle perfectly captures the essence of the book: it offers strategies to master interpersonal interactions. You'll discover strategies to get individuals from contemplation to action and from resistance to understanding, as well as techniques for motivating slackers to cooperate.

4. Robert B. Reich. Your Job is Change. 30 September
    2000.
    This is a blog post (long read) featured on Fast Company
    (www.fastcompany. com/41467/your-job-change). Become a
    change insurgent to transform your organization and engage
    others in it.

About the author

Susana Martínez Denia is an Executive Coach with more than 15 years of experience in the banking, professional services and people development sectors.

She shifted from quantitative models to people and founded Insatiable Leaders® – a coaching boutique firm specializing in elevating high-achieving leaders and forward-thinking organizations with an ongoing appetite for advancement.

Her devotion lies in harnessing the full potential of leaders' ideas, knowledge and talents, empowering them to excel in their careers, make a difference in their industries and companies, and inspire others in their environment to do the same.

Her focus is on exploring the unique qualities that differentiate leaders as catalysts of transformation and growth in organizations and creating coaching and training solutions to foster their development.

Susana works with leaders who aim to chart new growth thresholds for their business, themselves and others within their first 90 days in new leadership roles, as they pursue promotions and/or as they seek to drive change and expansion. Equally, she partners with talent specialists aiming to invigorate their leadership development initiatives to attract, develop and retain critical leaders and top talent.

Over the years, Susana has applied her three-pillar model to coach and train senior leaders in global organizations such as Goldman Sachs, EY, Meta, Google and PWC.

In her career, Susana has worked as a Chief Operating Officer and Career coach for a leading career-coaching company in London. Prior to becoming a coach, she led multicultural teams that provided advisory services for disputes relating to complex financial market issues and over-the-counter (OTC) derivatives valuation services for hedge funds.

Trilingual in English, Spanish and French, she holds a Master's Degree in Quantitative Finance and is a certified coach by the International Coach Federation and the Institute of Leadership and Management in the UK.

Susana can be reached at hello@insatiable-leaders.com

Acknowledgements: my environment

I would like to express my gratitude to my environment, the individuals who have supported me through the journey of nurturing the initiative of Insatiable Leaders® and have made this book possible.

Thank you to my parents who made me insatiable, gave the best insatiable partner in crime to grow with, my brother, and nurtured a home in which they cultivated our inquisitiveness, sense of possibilities and grit. Specially to my mother, for her unconditional support and encouragement, always balanced with a dose of challenge. To my father, for his endless optimism for life in general and enthusiasm about this project in particular. And to my brother, Fer, pure magic, who has literally made me stronger.

To my insatiable friends, Jenny, Cris and Agus, who were a source of motivation to start shaping this project back in 2017. Seeing you grow professionally and evolve in your careers and lives has been an inspiration in this journey.

To two other insatiable friendships that I found later in life and without whom this book could be still on the back burner: to Yuls, for crossing my path again and igniting possibilities and to Raúl, for his time, energy and enthusiasm to nurture this project.

To my unconditional cheerleaders, Elena, Nere, Lasa, Luis, Marta, Nat, Mel, Ana, Janis, Elsa and Nicole. To Fer the IV, for keeping me sane and laughing these last months. To Clara, for fuelling my motivation and also ideas for the manuscript. And to Nata, who has co-written many pages of my life.

To my beta readers, David, Richard, Pete, Laura, Vanisha, Alex, Ricardo and Mariví. Thank you for challenging me, championing me and advancing me in my thinking.

To my bright publisher, Alison Jones at Practical Inspiration Publishing, for her energy and inspirational standards. To Helen and Lesley, who led me to the finish line. To Ben Goia, for making me think that getting the ideas out of my mind was easy. And to the 53 leaders I interviewed in the summer of 2022.

To Adri, and a last-minute angel, María Diaz, Designer (@ mariadiazdesigner), who has perfected my drawings.

And lastly to my clients: you're the co-authors of this book. Thank you for enabling me to have access to your wonderful minds and souls. You make this journey worth it.

Notes

Chapter 1

[1] Douglas A. Ready, Jay A. Conger, and Linda A. Hill. Are You a High Potential? Harvard Business Review. June 2010. https://hbr.org/2010/06/are-you-a-high-potential

[2] Magellan got the credit, but Elcano was first to sail around the world. National Geographic. 1 September 2022. https://nationalgeographic.co.uk/history-and-civilisation/2022/09/magellan-got-the-credit-but-this-man-was-first-to-sail-around-the-world

[3] The original Olympic motto was 'Citius, Altius, Fortius' – 'Faster Higher, Stronger'. On 20 July 2021, it changed to 'Citius, Altius, Fortius – Communiter', which translates to 'Faster, Higher, Stronger –Together'. International Olympic Committee. https://olympics.com/ioc/olympic-motto

[4] What is the Olympic motto? International Olympic Committee. https://olympics.com/ioc/faq/olympic-symbol-and-identity/what-is-the-olympic-motto

[5] American Museum of Natural History. Einstein Exhibition. https://amnh.org/exhibitions/einstein/time/a-matter-of-time

[6] 'Faster, higher, further' is associated with Captain Marvel as it reflects the superhero's motto and encapsulates her journey and character traits.

[7] Robert Hargrove. *Masterful Coaching*. 2008, p. 119.

Chapter 2

[1] Sir Ken Robinson was a global authority on creativity, education and human potential, celebrated for his transformative TED Talk, 'Do Schools Kill Creativity?'

[2] Tony Robbins. What's key to being fulfilled in life? https://tonyrobbins.com/ask-tony/fulfillment/

Part II

[1] Inspired by Robert Hargrove's quote: 'Extraordinary leaders develop in the process of producing extraordinary results.' *Masterful Coaching*. 2008. Introduction, p. xvii.

Chapter 3

[1] Daniel Priestley. *Key Person of Influence* (revised edition). 2014. Constructing your presentation pitch, p. 90.

Chapter 4

[1] Doug Silsbee. *Presence-Based Coaching*. 2008, p. 41.

[2] Doug Silsbee. *Presence-Based Leadership*. 2018. The cascading on-ramp behaviour, pp. 140–141.

[3] Doug Silsbee. *Presence-Based Coaching*. 2008. How humans change, p. 45.

[4] Doug Silsbee. *Presence-Based Coaching*. 2008, p. 65.

[5] Doug Silsbee. *Presence-Based Coaching*. 2008, p. 46.

[6] Robert Hargrove. *Masterful Coaching*. 2008. Recognizing river and rut stories, pp. 122–123. He refers to rut and river stories, but I changed the name to box and breakthrough stories to align them with my explanation.

[7] Doug Silsbee. *Presence-Based Coaching*. 2008, p. 65.

Chapter 5

[1] Margaret Heffernan. Forget the pecking order at work. May 2015. www.ted.com/talks/margaret_heffernan_forget_the_pecking_order_at_work?hasProgress=true&language=en

Chapter 6

[1] The 'Eat The Frog' technique is a productivity and time management strategy that involves identifying your most difficult task of the day and completing it before you do any other work.

[2] Doug Silsbee. *Presence-Based Coaching*. 2008, pp. 21–25.

Index

achievement domain 39–41
Agricultural Revolution 9
anchoring 50
Aristotle 177
attachments 112–113, 123
   non-linear time management 181–182,
      186–187
attainment 49
attunement 49–51
aversions 112–113, 123
   non-linear time management 181–182,
      186–187

blind spots 55–56, 165
body awareness 120–123, 129, 193–194
box stories 118, 129
breakthrough stories 118–120, 129
breathing exercise 122, 193–194
Bushnell, Nolan 59

Chandler, Steve, *Time Warrior* 181
choices 50–51
Clear, James 132
coaching 141–142
   assessing team members 150–151
   model 142–148
   upgrade your identity 148–149
Cognitive Revolution 8, 9

competitive advantage 73, 79–83
Costolo, Dick 43
curiosity
   inside-out lens 26–30
   outside-in lens 26–28, 30
   see also endlessly curious and
      unstoppable learners

Deming, William Edwards 115
determination *see* self-reliant and
      determined
Duckworth, Angela, *Grit* 53

Einstein, Albert 4, 12–13
Elcano, Juan Sebastián 9–10
emotional (time) management 183,
      186–189
endlessly curious and unstoppable
      learners xix, 5–7, 10, 24–25, 67
   channelling 66
   double-edged sword: knowledge not
      translating into impact
      xxiv–xxv, 25–28
   shift: curiosity towards yourself 29–31
   trap: learning and your mind have
      become your comfort zone 28–29
engagement
   of others 86–87, 161–162

of yourself 87
environment 70–72, 131–132, 173–174
    as catapult 135, 172
    politics 159–160
        political moves 164–171
        transformation 160–163
    as propulsor 135, 172
    team of A-players 138–139
        coaching 141–151
        individuals' transformation
            139–141
    units of excellence 151–152
        bottom-up change 152–154
        group identity 154–159
    upgrade 56–58, 132–134
        complex systems 136–138
        victim vs catalyst 134–136
evolution 8–10
excellence *see* raise the bar and
        standards of excellence
expansiveness xxii–xxiii
expert positioning 73, 75, 80–86
explorers, insights from 9–10

Federer, Roger 106, 107
Flores, Fernando 128
focus 95–96, 100
    coaching 147–148
    declaring your vision 97–99
    drawing your vision 96–97
    linear time management 180
    presence 192, 194
frustrations, surfacing 7–8
future, speak from the 97–99, 100

grit 53

habit 109–112, 115, 128, 129
    loop 113, 115–118, 124, 128
    non-linear time management 182, 184
    presence 193–194
Harari, Yuval Noah, *Sapiens* 8–9

Hargrove, Robert 17–18
Heffernan, Margaret 157
high-performers (high-achievers)
        5–6
high-potentials 5–6
human evolution 8–10

identity 70–72, 103–104, 128–130
    environment 168
    group 154–155
        assessment 156–159
        dialogues and dynamics
            155–156
    meet your identity and the box it
        traps you in 107–108
        attachments and aversions
            112–113
        and habits 108–112
    need for change 104–107
    non-linear time management
        181–184, 187, 189–190
    ongoing elevation 125–128
    reinforce your new identity 123–125
    surface your identity 113–14
        winning strategies 114–116
    team of A-players 142, 144–146,
        148–149, 150
    upgrade 116–118
        body awareness 120–123
        box stories 118
        breakthrough stories 119–120
        coaching 148–149
impact xxi–xxii, xxiii, xxv, 15–17
    busyness vs 45–47
    knowledge not translating into
        xxiv–xxv, 25–28
    sense of urgency to step into the
        future 60–63
'impossibilities' 89, 98
imposter syndrome 33, 42
intellectual property (IP) 29
Ionesco, Eugène 146

Jobs, Steve 35, 74

Lao Tzu 104
leadership box 17–20
  identity 107–108, 126–127
    attachments and aversions
      112–113
    and habits 108–112
    reinforcement 125
    surfacing 114
    upgrade 117–119
learners *see* endlessly curious and
    unstoppable learners
linear time management 179–181

Magella, Ferdinand 9–10
Mandela, Nelson 95
Manson, Mark 185
mastery 196, 200
meta-abilities 176–178, 197–198, 200
  non-linear time management 176–
    181, 197
    emotional (time) management
      186–189
    identity 181–183
    strategic thinking time 189–190
    time deprivation 183–186
  presence 176–179, 190–191, 197
    cultivating 193–195
    mastery 196
    transformation 191–193
metrics
  distorted 41–43
  ownership 43–44
Michelangelo 88
momentum xxi–xxii, xxiv, xxv, 16–17
  busyness vs 45–47
  sense of urgency to step into the
    future 60–61
multitalented, ultra-capable and
    overscheduled xx, 5–7, 11,
    44–45, 67

channelling 66
double-edged sword: busyness is not
    performance, nor impact nor
    momentum xxv, 45–47
  shift: attune 50–51
  trap: you add but don't adjust 48–49

Nadal, Rafael 106–107, 114
Nadal, Toni, *Everything can be Trained*
    (*Todo se puede entrenar*)
    106–107
need for insatiable leadership xx–xxiii
non-linear time management 176–179,
    197
  emotional (time) management
    186–189
  identity 181–183
  strategic thinking time 189–190
  time deprivation 183–186

Olympic Movement 11
organizational aspirations 78–83, 85–86
  intersection with personal aspirations
    86–87
overscheduled *see* multitalented, ultra-
    capable and overscheduled
ownership of growth and metrics 43–44

partnership 147–148
performance xxi–xxii, xxiv, xxv, 15–17
  busyness vs 45–47
personal aspirations 78–80, 83–86
  intersection with organizational
    aspirations 86–87
pilots, small 169–170
pioneer leaders 92–93
  focus 98
pioneer visions 89–92, 101–102
  crafting 93–95
  focus 96, 98
politics 159–160, 173
  political moves 164–171

transformation 160–163
presence 176–179, 190–191, 197
  cultivating 193–195
  mastery 196
  transformation 191–193
Priestley, Daniel, *Key Person of Influence*
  101

question the limits *see* think big and
  question the limits

raise the bar and standards of excellence
  xix, 5–7, 11, 37–38, 67
  channelling 66
  double-edged sword: disconnect from
    what's meaningful xxv, 38–41
  shift: lean into significance and take
    ownership of your growth and
    metrics 43–44
  trap: drift into an unfulfilling
    quadrant and distorted metrics
    41–43
resourcefulness 98–99
Robbins, Tony 39

Scientific Revolution 9
self-generative loop 116–117, 127–129
self-reliant and determined xx, 5–7, 15,
  51–52, 67
  channelling 66
  double-edged sword: lean back from
    the environment you need to
    grow xxv, 53–55
  shift: lean in to upgrade your
    environment 56–58
  trap: difficult to question your blind
    spots 55–56
sense of urgency to step into the future
  xx, 5–7, 15, 58–59, 67
  channelling 66
  double-edged sword: sacrifice traction
    at scale in the system xx, 59–62

shift: create space and go into the
    fishbowl 63–65
  trap: resistance to suspend your
    motion and progression 62–63
significance domain 39–43
Silsbee, Doug 104, 111, 116
sports, insights from 11–12, 106–107,
  114
standards of excellence *see* raise the bar
  and standards of excellence
status quo
  perpetuating the 33–35
  questioning the xxv, 32–33
strategic thinking time 183, 188–190,
  198
  presence 194

team of A-players 138–139, 172
  assessment 150–151
  coaching 141–151
  individuals' transformation 139–141
think big and question the limits xix,
  5–7, 10, 31–32, 67
  channelling 66
  double-edged sword: question the
    status quo but question yourself
    xxv, 32–33
  shift: craft a vision that pulls you
    through obstacles 35–37
  trap: focus on the obstacles, play a
    smaller game and perpetuate
    the status quo 33–35
three-pillar model 70–72, 200
  see also environment; identity; vision
time bending 13–15
time deprivation 183–186
time management
  linear 179–181
  non-linear 176–179, 197
    emotional (time) management
    186–189
    identity 181–183

strategic thinking time 189–190
time deprivation 183–186
trampoline analogy 161–171
transactional interactions 141
transformational interactions 139–141

ultra-capable *see* multitalented, ultra-
capable and overscheduled
units of excellence 151–152, 172
bottom-up change 152–154
group identity 154–159
unstoppable learners *see* endlessly
curious and unstoppable
learners
urgency *see* sense of urgency to step
into the future

vision 35–37, 70–74, 100–102
focus 95–96, 100

declaring your vision 97–99
drawing your vision 96–97
identity 123–125
pioneer 96, 98
politics 161
push vs pull 74–78, 100, 144
stretch 88–89, 100
pioneer leaders 92–93
pioneer visions 89–92, 93–95,
101–102
take a stand 78–80, 94, 100
engagement to break through
barriers 86–87
organizational and personal
aspirations 80–86
team of A-players 142–144, 150

Wilde, Oscar 32
winning strategies 114–116, 128